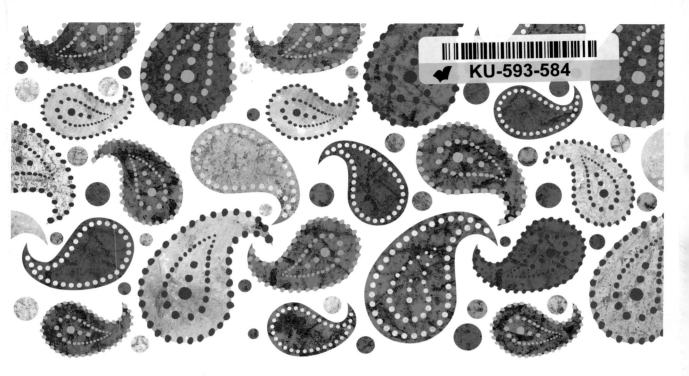

SABRINA GHAYOUR
FEASTS

MITCHELL
BEAZLEY

An Hachette UK Company
www.hachette.co.uk

First published in Great Britain in 2017 by Mitchell Beazley,
a division of Octopus Publishing Group Ltd
Carmelite House
50 Victoria Embankment
London EC4Y 0DZ
www.octopusbooks.co.uk

ISBN 9781784722135

A CIP catalogue record for this book is available from the British Library.

Printed and bound in China

10 9 8 7 6 5 4 3 2 1

Publishing Director Stephanie Jackson
Managing Editor Sybella Stephens
Copy Editor Salima Hirani
Creative Director Jonathan Christie
Senior Designer Jaz Bahra
Photographer Kris Kirkham
Illustrator Anna Koska
Food Stylist Laura Field
Food Stylist's Assistant Kim Somauroo
Prop Stylist Jenny Iggleden
Senior Production Manager Peter Hunt
Production Controller Sarah Kulasek-Boyd

FEASTS

'Life is a feast, and all who eat and drink with me,
and savour food as they savour life,
are those who matter most.'

CONTENTS

INTRODUCTION

As a child, growing up in a Persian household means endless parties, which we call *mehmooni*. My family regularly played host, and we would frequently attend big family gatherings, both indoors and outdoors. Those parties, and the feasts we shared at them, became a huge and influential part of my childhood. The overwhelming noise of people animatedly greeting one another as they embraced, and the loud infectious laughter and warmth that were shared are things I will never forget. I am so grateful to have been part of something that I now treasure as a golden era in my life.

I remember arriving at parties and being immediately seduced by the exotic smells that filled the house. I would watch platter after platter of elaborately presented dishes emerge from the kitchen, being carried carefully to the table. Once laid out, they would form part of an enormous, colourful spread that would soon be descended upon by dozens of people at once, yet seemed never-ending in supply. When you are a kid at only about table height, you have a major advantage over everyone else – sneaking away little bites before the grown-ups were ready to eat was not terribly uncommon in my case.

Feasting plays an important role not only in Persian culture but also in that of the entire Middle East. In ancient terms, what was served and how many exotic dishes and ingredients were offered might have sealed the fate of an entire empire! Feasts have always played an important role in the history of empires across the globe, and the breaking of bread and sharing of meals have long played a part in uniting cultures, communities and families by bringing people together in a convivial and uninhibited way, where all differences can be left aside at the table. Today, time plays a key factor in whether or not we entertain and we don't seem to entertain as often as we used to – life seems to get in the way.

I thought carefully about the types of recipes I wanted to share with you in this book and the chapters are dedicated to creating meals that are conducive to the way we live our lives today. I've suggested a menu within each chapter, but as the biggest rule breaker of them all, I am the kind of person who will choose a recipe from every chapter and throw them all together for a feast, so I would encourage you to make your own choices and do the same.

As is the case in my previous books, the recipes I offer are straightforward and, for the most part, not too labour-intensive (and, in some cases, really quite easy to make) but deliver big in the flavour sweepstakes, even if they contain only a handful of ingredients. It seems the older I get, the more I crave simplicity over refinement and fuss.

Many of you are now very familiar with the Middle East and its abundance of flavour, colour and ingredients. While my recipes are very much my own creations and the kind of food I like to eat at home, they remain heavily inspired by my travels and the wonderful produce and ingredients from around the world. There will always be plenty of Persian flavour inspiration to help you create a feast that is perfect for your table, no matter what the occasion may be.

The recipes in this book may be new but my ethos remains the same – no ingredient is truly ever essential (unless you are baking, when sometimes science takes precedence over creativity) and there is always room to chop and change ingredients and use what you have or what you can get hold of. In most cases, missing an ingredient won't affect the flavour or nature of a dish, so don't be afraid to skip or substitute an ingredient here or there. I realize how many people are afraid to deviate from a recipe for fear of failure, but I can assure you that I myself am not the type of cook who sticks to a recipe 100 per cent of the time, and generally it works, so don't be afraid to go off-piste.

Whether you follow my chapter and menu suggestions or if, like me, you prefer to pick and choose recipes from across the board to create your own special feast, may your feasts always be plentiful – I hope this book provides you with easy inspiration to make cooking less of a chore and more of a joy.

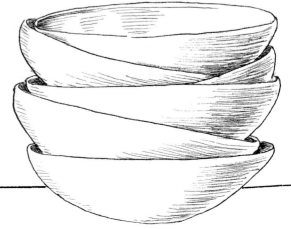

BREAKFAST
&
BRUNCH

It has long been said that breakfast is the most important meal of the day. Even the word itself, when broken down into 'break' and 'fast', reminds us of its actual purpose. Most of us will have our own preferences and rituals when we have a little more time on our hands rather than just enough time to smear a thin layer of spread across a piece of toast and fly out of the door with it dangling from our mouths.

I will let you in on a secret… I am a strange one when it comes to leisurely breakfast feasting, in that I need to start the day with a ritual of two cups of coffee, then some toast. Within a couple of hours, I am then ready for a heartier breakfast or brunch. So, basically, I am a two-breakfast kind of gal. Also, what I eat for breakfast is very much mood-driven. Consistency and necessity never play a role in my selections. I can hop erratically and wildly around the food groups and eat everything from leftover curry and roast potatoes to cold clams with chilli and garlic or just a piece of ham. I am aware this is not something most people do, but it does say something about my tastes – that I veer mostly towards savoury dishes for brunch.

When you have a family or group to feed for breakfast or brunch, you really want to put your energy and effort into making dishes that have interesting but not too many overpowering flavours, as subtlety goes a long way at this time of the day. Subtlety has many guises and need never be boring, familiar or predictable – I like to serve the kind of dishes that provide a wake-up-call, flavour-wise, to those who need it, and that set you up for the day, not just the morning, with flavours that are often bold but always balanced.

Choose one recipe or choose them all – there is something for everyone in this chapter, and you can throw in a few of your own favourite breakfast essentials. The point here is to take what you like and combine it with what you have and what your favourite staples are… that is always the winning formula for any great meal, no matter what time of day.

BREAKFAST & BRUNCH

MENU

Cheddar & feta frittata with peppers, herbs & pul biber (see page 18)

Sausage, potato, pepper & onion bake with yogurt & chilli sauce (see page 22)

Whipped ricotta & fig toasts with candied chilli bacon (see page 30)

Caramelized banana crêpes with pistachios & honey (see page 33)

Accompaniments:
Tea, coffee & fruit juice

GOATS' CHEESE & FILO PIES

with orange, pistachio & oregano

MAKES 8

100g pistachio nuts, finely chopped

400g soft goats' cheese

finely grated zest of 2 large unwaxed oranges

2 heaped teaspoons dried oregano

3 sheets of filo pastry

50g unsalted butter, melted, plus extra for greasing

1 tablespoon nigella seeds

clear honey, for drizzling (optional)

freshly ground black pepper

Preheat the oven to 220°C (200°C fan), Gas Mark 7. Grease an 8-hole muffin tin with melted butter.

Put the pistachios and goats' cheese into a large bowl. Add the orange zest, oregano and a generous amount of black pepper and mash together using a fork until the mixture is evenly combined. Divide the mixture equally into 8 portions.

Cut each filo pastry sheet roughly into 8 squares, each about 12cm square. Overlap 1 pastry square with another to make an 8-pointed star. Push the stars into 8 holes of the muffin tin and brush with melted butter. Spoon 1 portion of the filling into each pastry case and press gently on the filling.

Take 1 of the remaining pastry squares and crinkle it up in your hand. Place it on top of one of the pie fillings, brush with butter, then fold over the pastry edges to seal the pie. Brush the edges with more butter and sprinkle over a few nigella seeds. Repeat until all the pies are topped and sealed.

Bake for about 25 minutes, or until deeply golden brown. Drizzle each pie with a little clear honey if desired, then serve.

CHEDDAR & FETA FRITTATA

with peppers, herbs & pul biber

SERVES 4–6

vegetable oil

½ red pepper, cut into 1cm strips, then diced into 1cm pieces

½ green pepper, cut into 1cm strips, then diced into 1cm pieces

4 spring onions, thinly sliced from root to tip

200g feta cheese, broken off into 1cm chunks

100g mature Cheddar cheese, grated

1 tablespoon pul biber chilli flakes

½ small bunch (about 15g) of dill, finely chopped

½ small bunch (about 15g) of fresh coriander, finely chopped

8 large eggs, beaten

Maldon sea salt flakes and freshly ground black pepper

Preheat the oven to 220°C (200°C fan), Gas Mark 7.

Drizzle a little oil into a large, ovenproof frying pan and set it over a medium-high heat. When the oil is hot, add the peppers and fry for 1 minute, stirring to prevent them from taking on colour or burning. Mix in the spring onions, feta, Cheddar, pul biber, dill and coriander.

Season the beaten eggs well with salt and pepper and pour them over the ingredients in the pan, then shake the pan to ensure the egg spreads evenly around the pan and coats all the contents. Cook for about 2 minutes, or until you see the edges of the frittata begin to solidify, then transfer the pan to the oven and bake for 10–12 minutes, or until the frittata is cooked – insert a knife into the centre to ensure the egg is cooked through. Either slide or flip the frittata on to a plate and serve – or eat straight from the pan. Leftovers are great served at room temperature.

SPICY TAMARIND BEANS

500g dried haricot beans

2–3 tablespoons vegetable oil

2 large onions, finely chopped or minced
in a food processor

2 fat garlic cloves, crushed

1 tablespoon cocoa powder

2 teaspoons ground cinnamon

2 teaspoons ground cumin

1 teaspoon cayenne pepper

400g can chopped tomatoes

100g tamarind paste (the paste should
be the consistency of a ketchup)

4 tablespoons brown sugar

4 tablespoons red wine vinegar

500ml boiling water

Maldon sea salt flakes and freshly ground
black pepper

toasted bread, to serve

Soak the beans overnight, then drain and rinse well. Transfer the beans to a large saucepan, cover with cold water and boil over a medium-high heat for about 45 minutes, or until just tender. Drain and rinse well to remove excess starch.

Heat the oil in a large saucepan over a medium-high heat. Add the onions and fry for 6–8 minutes, or until translucent and the edges start to brown. Add the beans, garlic, cocoa powder and spices and stir to coat the beans well. Next add the canned tomatoes, tamarind paste, sugar and red wine vinegar and season generously. Pour in the 500ml of boiling water, reduce the heat to low and simmer for 1–1½ hours, or until the beans are soft (taste a bean to check). Check the seasoning and adjust to your taste.

Serve with toasted bread. This dish is great served with bacon or sausages.

TIP

Tamarind paste comes in different consistencies and concentrates. This recipe is best made with a paste the consistency of thick ketchup – it should not be dense or sticky. If your paste is the thicker more concentrated variety, simply add less of it and more sweetness to balance the flavours and to suit your preference.

SAUSAGE, POTATO, PEPPER & ONION BAKE

with yogurt & chilli sauce

SERVES 4-6

2 teaspoons cumin seeds

2 teaspoons coriander seeds

1 tablespoon sweet paprika

2 tablespoons pul biber chilli flakes

500g sausages (preferably with a high meat content)

3 tablespoons garlic oil

2 large potatoes, parboiled with skin on and cut into 1cm-thick slices

200g small peppers or 1 large red and 1 large green pepper, cored, deseeded and cut lengthways into 2.5cm-thick strips

2 large red onions, quartered and each quarter halved

Maldon sea salt flakes and freshly ground black pepper

TO SERVE
200g thick Greek yogurt
your favourite chilli sauce

Heat a large frying pan over a medium-high heat, add the cumin and coriander seeds and dry-toast for about 1 minute, shaking the pan until they release their aroma and begin to brown a little, taking care not to let them burn. Using a pestle and mortar, crush the seeds very roughly, just to break them. Transfer to a bowl and combine with the paprika and pul biber.

Set the same frying pan you used to toast the seeds over a high heat and fry the sausages for 6–8 minutes, or until they start to brown on all sides – you don't need to fully cook them in the pan as they will finish cooking in the oven later. Cut each sausage into 3 slices diagonally and set aside.

Preheat the oven to its highest temperature. Line a large baking tray with baking paper.

Brush the paper with 1 tablespoon of the garlic oil and season the base with salt and pepper. Lay the potato slices in the tray and season again with salt and pepper and one-third of the spice mixture. Evenly distribute the sausages, peppers and onions in the tray. Reserve a little of the spice mix for sprinkling, then drizzle over the remaining garlic oil and spice mix and season generously with salt and pepper.

Bake for 16–18 minutes, or until the peppers are nicely browned and the sausages are cooked through.

Serve with dollops of thick Greek yogurt, a good drizzle of your favourite chilli sauce (I love sriracha) and a sprinkling of the remaining spice mix. This dish goes well with simple fried or scrambled eggs.

GREEN GINGER LEMONADE

SERVES 4

ice cubes

1 small bunch (about 30g) of mint,
  stalks removed

½ small bunch (about 15g) of dill,
  roughly chopped

5cm piece of fresh root ginger,
  peeled and very finely chopped

6 tablespoons caster sugar,
  plus extra to tasted

finely grated zest and juice of 3 lemons

1 litre tepid water

Fill a blender half full with ice cubes and add the mint leaves, dill, ginger, sugar, lemon zest and juice along with 500ml of the tepid water. Blitz until the mixture is well blended.

Transfer the liquid to a large jug, add the remaining water and stir. Check the sweetness and adjust to taste.

Put some ice cubes into 4 highball glasses, top up with the green lemonade and serve.

ZA'ATAR-CRUMBED
HALLOUMI

SERVES 4–5

vegetable oil

2 x 250g block of halloumi cheese

1 large egg, beaten

6 tablespoons fine, dried, natural
  breadcrumbs

4 tablespoons za'atar

Pour enough oil into a large, deep-sided frying pan to fill it to a depth of about 2.5cm. Heat the oil over a high heat. Line a plate with a double layer of kitchen paper.

Slice each block of halloumi into 5 even slices, each about 1cm thick. Put the beaten egg into a shallow bowl. Mix the breadcrumbs with the za'atar in a bowl. Dip each slice of halloumi into the egg to give it a generous coating, then roll it in the spiced breadcrumbs. When fully coated on all sides, fry the halloumi in the hot oil for about 1 minute, or until the crumbs turn golden brown. Transfer to the paper-lined plate to drain the excess oil, then serve immediately.

PEA PASTIZZI

MAKES 10

olive oil
1 large onion, very finely chopped
2 fat garlic cloves, crushed
300g can marrowfat peas
1 tablespoon medium-spiced curry powder
½ teaspoon freshly ground black pepper
20g unsalted butter
1 sheet of ready-rolled all-butter puff pastry
1 large egg, beaten
Maldon sea salt flakes

Drizzle a little olive oil into a frying pan set over a medium-high heat. When the oil is hot, add the onion and cook for a few minutes, until softened and starting to colour around the edges. Add the garlic and cook for about 1 minute, or until the onion and garlic begin to colour and are cooked through. Stir in the peas, curry powder, pepper, butter and a generous amount of salt (as peas are very sweet and need to be seasoned well). Cook for about 5 minutes, mashing the peas roughly as you stir, until they are cooked through. Remove the pan from the heat and leave to cool.

Preheat the oven to 200°C (180°C fan), Gas Mark 6. Line a large baking tray with baking paper.

Place the sheet of puff pastry on a clean work surface with its paper lining underneath it. Divide the sheet into 10 equal rectangles. Divide the cooled pea mixture into 10 sausage-shaped portions. Press 1 portion on to each rectangle of pastry. Gather the 2 ends of the pastry rectangle and fold them over the ends of the sausage, then roll up the filling in the pastry and pinch the pastry to seal in the filling. Seal any gaps in the pastry by carefully pinching them shut. Place the roll on the prepared baking tray with the sealed side facing downwards. Repeat with the remaining pastry rectangles and portions of filling. Brush the rolls with egg wash and bake for about 25 minutes, or until crisp and golden. Serve immediately. These rolls are also great served at room temperature.

APPLE, CINNAMON & SULTANA LOAF

with nigella honey butter

MAKES 1 LARGE LOAF

7g sachet of fast-action dried yeast

80ml lukewarm water

110ml milk, at room temperature

1 egg

75g caster sugar

75g sultanas

1 heaped tablespoon ground cinnamon

60g unsalted butter, melted, plus extra for greasing

1 Braeburn apple, coarsely grated

pinch of Maldon sea salt flakes

475g strong bread flour, plus extra as required

FOR THE NIGELLA HONEY BUTTER

2 tablespoons nigella seeds

100g unsalted butter

3 tablespoons clear honey

Dissolve the yeast in the lukewarm water and leave for 10 minutes to activate.

Put the milk, egg, sugar, sultanas, cinnamon, 40g of the melted butter, grated apple and salt into a large mixing bowl and mix well. Stir in the activated yeast liquid, then add the flour. Blend until a slightly sticky dough is formed. Use a little extra flour to help you bring the dough together, then knead it for a couple of minutes. Put the dough into a bowl, cover it with a clean tea towel and leave it somewhere warm to rest for 1½ hours.

To make the nigella honey butter, blitz the nigella seeds using a spice grinder or food processor until fine, or grind them using a pestle and mortar. Put the butter into a bowl, add the nigella seeds powder and honey and work them into the butter until evenly combined. Refrigerate until 15 minutes before needed.

When the resting time has elapsed, lightly grease a 900g loaf tin (21 x 11 x 7cm). Carefully remove the dough (using a little flour to extract it from the bowl, if needed) and shape it into a long loaf. Tuck the 2 long edges underneath so the top forms a smooth dome. Gently push the dough into the prepared tin and leave to prove (uncovered) in a warm place for 20 minutes.

Preheat the oven to 200°C (180°C fan), Gas Mark 6.

When the dough has risen in the tin, brush it with the remaining melted butter. Bake for 45–50 minutes, or until the top is deeply golden brown and the loaf sounds hollow when tapped. Remove from the tin and allow to cool completely, then serve the loaf with the nigella honey butter.

WHIPPED RICOTTA
& FIG TOASTS

with candied chilli bacon

MAKES 4

200g thick-cut unsmoked streaky bacon
(approximately 14 slices)

1 tablespoon pul biber chilli flakes,
plus extra to serve

4 tablespoons clear honey

200g ricotta cheese

1 heaped teaspoon dried thyme,
plus extra to serve

zest of 1 unwaxed orange

4 large slices of sourdough bread

4 figs, each cut into 5–6 segments

Maldon sea salt flakes and freshly ground
black pepper

Heat a large frying pan over a high heat. Line a plate with a double layer of kitchen paper.

When the frying pan is hot, add the bacon and dry-fry for a few minutes on each side, until the fat has rendered and the bacon is golden brown, completely crisp and can be crumbled with ease. Transfer to the paper-lined plate to drain excess oil. When dry, crumble the bacon into a small bowl and crush it finely with a fork. Mix in the pul biber and honey and set aside.

Put the ricotta, dried thyme and orange zest into a large bowl, season generously with salt and pepper and whip until smooth and a little aerated.

Toast the bread, then divide the ricotta mixture between the slices. Reserve a little of the bacon mixture for sprinkling, then divide the remaining mixture into 4 portions and spoon 1 portion over the ricotta on each slice of bread. Arrange the fig slices on top, then sprinkle over the reserved bacon and a little dried thyme and pul biber to serve.

CARAMELIZED BANANA CRÊPES

with pistachios & honey

MAKES 12

100g plain flour, sifted

pinch of salt

2 eggs

200ml milk

50ml water

50g salted butter, melted, plus an extra
    6 tablespoons

1 heaped tablespoon golden caster sugar

FOR THE TOPPING

3–4 tablespoons golden caster sugar

3 large or 4 small bananas, diagonally
    sliced 2.5cm thick

50g salted butter

75g pistachio nuts, roughly chopped

clear honey

To make the crêpe batter, put the flour, salt and eggs into a large mixing bowl. Combine the milk and measured water in a jug, then blend the liquid into the flour mixture a little at a time, whisking well with either a fork or an electric hand whisk to beat out any lumps. Mix in the 2 tablespoons of melted butter and the sugar, then transfer the mixture to a measuring jug and set aside.

Set a heatproof plate over a pan of simmering water – you can keep the cooked crêpes warm by stacking them on this plate as you cook them.

Heat an 18cm-diameter frying pan over a medium-high heat. Drizzle in 1 teaspoon of the melted butter and tilt the pan to spread it around the base of the pan. Quickly pour in just enough crêpe batter to barely coat the base (you want a nice, thin crêpe, not a pancake) and tilt the pan to spread the batter evenly. Cook for about 1 minute, or until the edges start to curl up, then use a knife to tease the edge of the crêpes over to check if the underside is golden and, if so, flip the crêpe (use a spatula if you like) and cook for a further 30 seconds or so, until the underside is golden brown. Transfer the crêpe to the warm plate and cover with greaseproof paper. Repeat with the remaining batter, adding 1 teaspoon melted butter to the pan each time. Keep the crêpes warm while you cook the topping.

Put the caster sugar into a shallow dish. Dip the 2 cut sides of each banana slice into the sugar to coat.

Put 25g of the butter into a large frying pan set over a high heat. Add half the banana slices and fry for no more than 1 minute on each side, or until slightly caramelized. Remove from the pan and repeat with the remaining butter and banana slices.

To serve, place a few banana slices across half of each crêpe. Scatter over the pistachios and drizzle a little honey over each. Fold into quarters and serve immediately.

SPICED CHAI-FROSTED CUPCAKES

MAKES 12

FOR THE CAKES

3 aromatic tea bags such as Earl Grey, Darjeeling or English Breakfast

4 tablespoons boiling water

200ml milk

2 large eggs

75g unsalted butter, softened

250g caster sugar

225g plain flour

1 tablespoon baking powder

1 heaped teaspoon ground cinnamon

1 heaped teaspoon ground ginger

good pinch of salt

FOR THE FROSTING

50ml milk

pinch of ground cloves

seeds from 4 cardamom pods, finely ground using a pestle and mortar

1 teaspoon ground cinnamon

500g icing sugar

160g unsalted butter, softened

2 tablespoons dried edible rose petals, finely ground to a powder using a pestle and mortar or spice grinder

Put the tea bags into a bowl, add the 4 tablespoons of boiling water, then leave to infuse for 30 minutes.

Preheat the oven to 190°C (170°C fan), Gas Mark 5. Line a 12-hole muffin tin with paper muffin cases.

In a measuring jug, whisk the milk and eggs together, then pour in the infused tea. Squeeze out every last drop of tea from the tea bags without bursting them. Place the used tea bags in a small bowl with the milk for the frosting, ground cloves, cardamom and cinnamon and leave to steep for at least 1 hour.

Put the butter, sugar, flour, baking powder, cinnamon, ginger and salt into a large mixing bowl and combine slowly using an electric hand whisk on a low speed until the mixture is evenly mixed.

Pour half the milk, egg and tea mixture into the cake mixture and continue to blend on a low speed, then increase the speed and whisk until the mixture becomes nice and thick. Add the remaining milk, egg and tea mixture and whisk until smooth.

Divide the cake mixture between the muffin cases, filling 1cm from the tops of the cases. Bake for about 20 minutes, until nicely risen. Leave to cool in the tin for a few minutes, then transfer to a wire rack and leave to cool completely.

To make the frosting, remove the tea bags from the spiced milk mixture. Squeeze to extract all the flavour from the tea bags, then discard.

Put the icing sugar and butter into a mixing bowl. Using an electric hand whisk on a low speed, combine until smooth, then add the spiced milk and continue to whisk, increasing the speed gradually, until the frosting is light and creamy.

Frost the cooled cakes by swirling the frosting with a small palette knife, then sprinkle each with rose petal powder.

WEEKEND
FEASTS

I think many of us often spend the whole week looking forward to the weekend, only to reach the weekend and find its appeal wears off because you end up stuck in the kitchen for most of it. There are ways to enjoy your time in the kitchen without having to spend the entire weekend slaving away.

While it's always nice to whip up a feast midweek, sometimes, between the constraints of work and family life, it can all get a bit much. It's on the weekends that some of my best cooking is done. I find the relaxed, unhurried pace allows me to put a little more thought into the dish I'm preparing and I get a lot more joy out of what I serve.

Many of us meet friends and family over the weekends, and sometimes – if you don't plan things carefully – you can end up regretting the decision to play host. And more importantly, you can easily miss out on valuable downtime spent enjoying the fruits of your labour. I realize that you may not want to spend a whole day cooking, but you still want to serve satisfying and impressive meals. With that in mind, I've put together this chapter of recipes that come together easily and that – with a little planning – enable you to enjoy more time around the table and less time toiling away in the kitchen. Some of the recipes can be scaled up to feed surprise visitors, so you can turn out weekend food that is delicious and perfect for sharing.

WEEKEND FEASTS

—

MENU

Chicken, pistachio & black pepper curry (see page 42)

Coriander, lime & garlic rice (see page 49)

Pomegranate & aubergine salad with harissa & sun-dried tomatoes (see page 52)

Tomato & olive salad with za'atar & a buttermilk dressing (see page 57)

Peach, lime & pistachio polenta cake (see page 63)

Accompaniment:
Mint tea mojitos (see page 64)

CHICKEN, PISTACHIO &
BLACK PEPPER CURRY

SERVES 6

2 tablespoons vegetable oil

2 onions, roughly chopped

800g boneless, skinless chicken thigh fillets

2 tablespoons coarse black pepper

a large bunch (about 50g) fresh coriander, roughly chopped, plus extra leaves to garnish

seeds from 6 green cardamom pods

2 long red chillies

7.5cm piece of fresh root ginger, peeled and roughly chopped

5 fat garlic cloves

100g pistachio nuts

300g peeled and deseeded butternut squash, cut into 5cm-long, 2.5cm-thick chunks

150g baby sweetcorn

Maldon sea salt flakes

rice or naan bread, to serve

Heat the oil in a large saucepan over a medium-high heat. Add the onions and fry for 6–8 minutes, or until translucent and the edges start to brown. Add the chicken and black pepper and seal the chicken by cooking for about 1 minute on all exposed sides, taking care not to let the chicken brown.

Put the coriander, cardamom seeds, chillies, ginger, garlic and pistachios into a blender with enough water to cover them all. Blend until the mixture is evenly green and silky-smooth with no lumps.

When the chicken is sealed, stir it well, then stir in the pistachio curry paste. Pour in just enough cold water to cover the chicken and paste mixture. Season generously with salt, and cook over a low heat for 1 hour.

Check the seasoning, ans add more salt if needed, then stir in the butternut squash and baby sweetcorn. Increase the heat to medium and cook for a further 30 minutes, or until the butternut squash and corn are both cooked and soft. Garnish with coriander leaves and serve with rice or toasted naan bread.

TIP

You can also use bone-in chicken thighs – discard the skin and add an additional 30 minutes to the cooking time before adding the vegetables.

SAVOURY PORK & FENNEL BAKLAVA

with roasted tomatoes & feta

MAKES 9 SQUARES

1kg pork shoulder or 1.3kg bone-in pork shoulder (leftover roast pork, lamb or chicken also works well)

400g cherry tomatoes, halved

2 tablespoons fennel seeds

olive oil

1 large onion, thinly sliced into half-moons

2 fat garlic cloves, crushed

400ml passata

4 tablespoons clear honey

75g unsalted butter, melted

6 sheets of filo pastry

200g feta cheese, crumbled

Maldon sea salt flakes and freshly ground black pepper

1 tablespoon nigella seeds, to garnish

FOR THE SYRUP

200ml boiling water

300g caster sugar

zest of 1 unwaxed orange

good pinch of cayenne pepper (optional)

Preheat the oven to 160°C (140°C fan), Gas Mark 3.

Put the pork into a roasting tray. Season the pork all over with a generous amount of salt and pepper. Put the pork into the oven on a high shelf, and roast for 3½–4 hours, covering the joint with kitchen foil for the final hour of cooking. Leave to cool in the tray.

Meanwhile line a baking tray with baking paper or silicone. Put the cherry tomato halves with their cut sides facing upwards on the prepared tray. Roast the tomatoes on a lower oven shelf under the pork for about 1¾ hours, or until nicely burnished around the edges. Leave to cool on the baking tray.

Pick all the meat from the cooled joint and discard the fat and any skin. Shred the meat lightly with a knife and set aside.

Heat a large frying pan over a medium-high heat, add the fennel seeds and dry-toast for about 1 minute, shaking the pan until they release their aroma and begin to brown a little, taking care not to let them burn. Add a generous drizzle of olive oil, then add the onions and fry for 5–6 minutes, or until translucent and the edges start to brown. Stir in the garlic and shredded pork, then the passata, honey and a generous amount of salt and pepper. Stir well, reduce the heat to medium-low and simmer gently for a few minutes, or until the sauce has reduced to a gravy-like consistency. Do not allow the sauce to become too dry – you want it to have a bit of moisture for a baklava. Take the pan off the heat and leave to cool until the mixture is just warm.

Preheat the oven to 200°C (180°C fan), Gas Mark 6. Brush the base of a 25–30cm square cake tin or ovenproof dish generously with some of the melted butter.

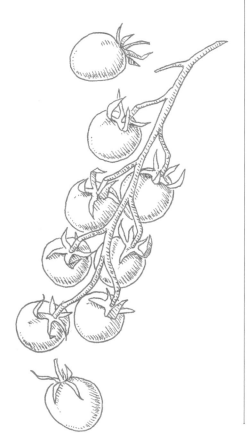

Line the base of the prepared tin with 4 sheets of filo pastry –
2 lengthways, 2 widthways – allowing an equal amount of
pastry to overhang each side of the tin. Brush the pastry with
melted butter. Spoon half the pork mixture into the tin and
spread it evenly across the pastry. Scatter over half the cherry
tomatoes and half of the crumbled feta. Fold 1 of the remaining
pastry sheets to make a rough square shape and use to cover the
layer of filling. Brush the pastry layer with butter. Now repeat the
process using the remaining pork mixture, tomatoes and feta.

Fold over the overhanging pastry and brush with melted
butter. Take the remaining pastry sheet, fold it into a square
shape slightly larger than the surface and cover the top. Tuck
the pastry edges down the sides of the tin using a round-bladed
knife or similar, then brush the top liberally with the remaining
butter. Using a very sharp knife, cut the top layers of pastry as
neatly as possible either into 9 squares or, by cutting in diagonal
lines, into diamond shapes (do this now, as it will be impossible
to cut neatly after cooking). Bake for 30 minutes, or until deep
golden brown.

Meanwhile, make the syrup. Put the 200ml of boiling water
into a small saucepan set over a medium-high heat, then add
the caster sugar and dissolve it in the hot water. Add the orange
zest and cayenne pepper, stir well, then simmer gently for
10–15 minutes, or until the mixture reduces to a syrup and can
coat the back of a spoon.

When the baklava is cooked, remove it from the oven and
immediately pour the syrup evenly over the top, then scatter
over the nigella seeds to garnish. Leave for 15 minutes to absorb
the syrup before serving. To serve, either remove the whole
baklava from the tin using a fish slice, transfer to a serving
platter and cut it at the table, or cut out individual portions
straight from the tin and serve with a green salad.

PAN-FRIED LAMB STEAKS, PRESERVED LEMON, CORIANDER & GARLIC

SERVES 4–6

6–8 thin cut lamb leg steaks
 (about 125g each)

FOR THE MARINADE
4 fat garlic cloves, bashed and thinly sliced
a small bunch (about 30g) of fresh
 coriander, finely chopped
6 preserved lemons, deseeded and
 finely chopped
1 tablespoon coarse black pepper
4–5 tablespoons olive oil
Maldon sea salt flakes

Put the garlic, coriander, preserved lemons and black pepper into a small bowl and season with just a little salt (as the preserved lemons are quite salty). Add the oil and mix well.

Put the lamb steaks into a large food bag and pour the marinade into the bag (alternatively, divide the lamb between 2 smaller food bags and add half the marinade to each bag). Seal the bag, then use your hands to work the marinade into the meat. Marinate at room temperature for a minimum of 20 minutes (although you can do this for a few hours in the refrigerator, too).

Set a large frying pan over a medium-high heat. When hot, add the steaks and fry for about 6 minutes on each side, ensuring they are nicely coated with a little of the marinade. Leave to rest for a few minutes before serving. This should give you beautifully cooked pink lamb steaks.

CORIANDER, LIME & GARLIC RICE

SERVES 4–6

a large bunch (about 50g) of fresh
 coriander, roughly chopped
6 fat garlic cloves, crushed
6 large lime leaves, cut into strips
finely grated zest and juice of 1 unwaxed lime
750ml cold water
2 heaped teaspoons coriander seeds
2 heaped teaspoons mustard seeds
olive oil
500g basmati rice
75g unsalted butter
Maldon sea salt flakes

In a blender, blitz the fresh coriander, garlic, lime leaves and lime zest and juice together with 250ml of the water. Once blended, stir in the remaining water and set aside.

Heat a large frying pan over a medium-high heat, add the mustard and coriander seeds and dry-toast for about 1 minute, shaking the pan until they release their aroma and begin to brown a little, taking care not to let them burn. Drizzle a little olive oil into the saucepan and stir in the rice, coating it well with the oil and spices. Add the butter. When melted, pour in the herb liquid, season generously with salt flakes, stir and cover the pan with a lid. Simmer for 20–25 minutes, or until the liquid has been absorbed. Fluff the rice with a fork before serving.

SPICED GARLIC
SAVOY CABBAGE RIBBONS

SERVES 4–6

1 large head of savoy cabbage (or your favourite green, leafy cabbage), halved, core removed and leaves cut into 2.5cm-thick ribbons

2 teaspoons cumin seeds

2 teaspoons coriander seeds

2 teaspoons mustard seeds

2 teaspoons nigella seeds

1–2 teaspoons chilli flakes, to taste

olive oil

1 whole head of garlic, cloves bashed and thinly sliced

50g unsalted butter, cut into cubes

6 tablespoons Greek yogurt

Maldon sea salt flakes and freshly ground black pepper

Wash and drain the cabbage ribbons, but do not shake off all the water as this will help to steam the cabbage later on.

Heat a large frying pan over a medium-high heat, add the spices and dry-toast for about 1 minute, shaking the pan until they release their aroma and begin to brown a little, taking care not to let them burn.

Drizzle in just enough olive oil to coat the base of the pan. Add the garlic and fry for 1 minute, then pack half of the cabbage into the pan. Season this layer with a little salt and pepper and stir well. Add the remaining cabbage, season this top layer with salt and pepper, then add a little drizzle of oil. Cover the pan with a lid and cook for 3–4 minutes without removing the lid – instead, hold the lid on firmly and shake the pan to move the cabbage around and prevent it from sticking. This enables the cabbage to fry and steam-cook at the same time.

Stir the cabbage well, ensuring the spices coat the cabbage, then add the butter and stir. Check and adjust the seasoning, then remove the pan from the heat. Stir in the yogurt and serve immediately.

POMEGRANATE &
AUBERGINE SALAD

with harissa & sun-dried tomatoes

SERVES 6–8

250–300ml vegetable oil

2–3 large or 5 small aubergines, cut into 5cm chunks

2 tablespoons olive oil

150ml pomegranate molasses

1 heaped tablespoon rose harissa

2–3 tablespoons clear honey, plus extra to taste

2 heaped tablespoons tomato purée

2 slices of day-old sourdough bread (if using fresh, briefly toast and leave to dry for 1 hour), cut into cubes

150g sun-dried tomatoes in oil, drained and cut widthways into strips

1 small bunch (about 30g) of flat leaf parsley, finely chopped

200g pomegranate seeds

100g pistachio nuts

Maldon sea salt flakes

Pour the vegetable oil into a large, deep saucepan and heat over a medium-high heat. Line a plate with a double layer of kitchen paper. Add the aubergines to the hot oil in the pan and fry for 10–15 minutes, stirring every few minutes to prevent burning, until fully cooked and deeply golden brown on all sides. Remember that aubergines need plenty of oil to cook properly, so add more oil if the pan becomes dry. Using a metal slotted spoon, transfer the cooked aubergine pieces to the paper-lined plate. Place another 2 sheets of kitchen paper on top and press the aubergine pieces gently with the paper to extract all excess oil. Leave to cool.

Put the olive oil into a large mixing bowl with the pomegranate molasses, harissa, honey and tomato purée and mix well. Add the stale bread cubes and coat them well with the mixture. Add the cooled aubergines, sun-dried tomatoes, parsley, pomegranate seeds and pistachios and season well with salt. Mix thoroughly. At this point, you can add more honey to balance out the sour notes to your taste. Cover the bowl with clingfilm and leave the salad to stand at room temperature for 30 minutes. This can also be made the day before and refrigerated overnight. Stir well before serving.

TIP

Don't be afraid about using this amount of oil to cook the aubergines – the excess oil can be squeezed out after cooking. To serve this as bruschetta, simply omit the bread from the recipe and serve on slices of toasted sourdough.

CELERIAC, ORANGE & CARAWAY SALAD

with a mustard yogurt dressing

SERVES 6–8

1 small celeriac or ½ very large one (exact
quantity does not matter)

1 small bunch (about 30g) of flat leaf
parsley, roughly chopped

2 teaspoons caraway seeds

150–200ml Greek yogurt (depending on
the quantity of celeriac)

2 heaped tablespoons Dijon mustard
(with or without seeds)

1 tablespoon olive oil

2 unwaxed oranges

Maldon sea salt flakes and freshly ground
black pepper

Peel the celeriac and cut it into manageable chunks (3 usually
works). Either grate them on the coarse plate of a box grater
or shred them in a food processor using the shredding plate.
Transfer to a mixing bowl. Reserve some of the chopped parsley
for the garnish. Add the chopped parsley, caraway seeds,
yogurt, mustard and olive oil to the bowl and stir well until
evenly combined. Finely grate the zest of the oranges directly
into the bowl and mix again. Season with salt and pepper to taste.

To peel the zested oranges, use a small, sharp knife to cut
away the top and bottom of the fruit. Rest the orange on the
cut surface, then slice away strips of peel and pith to expose
the flesh all around the orange. Halve each orange across the
middle and cut into half-moons, then halve those half-moons.
Add the orange pieces to the celeriac and fold them in gently
so as not to crush them. Serve immediately scattered with the
reserved chopped parsley.

TOMATO & OLIVE SALAD

with za'atar & a buttermilk dressing

SERVES 6–8

800g mixed tomatoes (any colours and varieties you can find)

250g pitted mixed olives or 300g if not pitted (I like using Kalamata or a nice firm green olive like Halkidiki)

15g chives, snipped

200ml buttermilk

olive oil (try a flavoured oil such as garlic or lemon oil)

2 tablespoons za'atar

Maldon sea salt flakes and freshly ground black pepper

Slice the tomatoes horizontally into 1cm-thick slices and arrange them on a large platter. Dot the platter with olives and scatter over half the snipped chives. Season generously with salt and pepper.

Season the buttermilk well with salt and a good slug of olive oil, then drizzle the buttermilk dressing over the salad. Scatter over the remaining chives and sprinkle over the za'atar. Serve immediately.

PRESERVED PEPPERS

stuffed with goats' cheese & pine nuts

400g jar piquant preserved or brined whole mini red peppers (I use Peppadew)

300–400g soft goats' cheese

finely grated zest of 2 unwaxed lemons

1 heaped teaspoon dried mint

1 small bunch (about 30g) of mint, leaves finely chopped

75g toasted pine nuts, roughly chopped

freshly ground black pepper

Drain the peppers carefully and pat them dry with kitchen paper.

Put the goats' cheese, lemon zest, dried and fresh mint and pine nuts into a bowl, season generously with black pepper and mix with a fork until evenly combined.

The fastest way to fill the peppers with the mixture is to use a piping bag fitted with a wide nozzle and pipe the mixture into each pepper. However, I confess I usually just fill the peppers carefully using a teaspoon, and wipe off any smudges of cheese from each pepper with kitchen paper.

Serve the stuffed peppers immediately or refrigerate until ready to serve later in the day, or even the following day.

PEAR & THYME TART

SERVES 6–8

1 sheet of ready-rolled all-butter puff pastry

2 large conference pears, peeled, halved, cored and thinly sliced

small handful of thyme leaves

2 heaped tablespoons golden caster sugar

½ teaspoon ground cinnamon

FOR THE CUSTARD

175ml double cream

2 egg yolks

1½ teaspoons vanilla bean paste

2 tablespoons thick strained Greek yogurt

1 tablespoon plain flour

1 heaped tablespoon thyme leaves, roughly chopped

2 tablespoons golden caster sugar

Preheat the oven to 210°C (190°C fan), Gas Mark 6½. Line a large baking tray with baking paper.

To make the custard, combine the cream, egg yolks, vanilla bean paste, yogurt and flour in a bowl and lightly beat with a whisk until it is evenly whipped and is the consistency of smooth, thick yogurt.

Using a pestle and mortar, pound the roughly chopped thyme leaves with the sugar until you have a smooth, thyme-infused sugar. Add the sugar to the custard mix and stir in until the mixture is very smooth and evenly combined.

Lay the unrolled puff pastry sheet in the prepared baking tray. Score a 2.5cm border around the edge of the pastry sheet and pour the custard mixture into the centre. Carefully spread it out to the edge of the scored border. Lay the pear slices, diagonally overlapping each other, over the custard to cover it. Scatter over the thyme leaves and also the golden caster sugar, then top with a scant sprinkle of cinnamon. Bake for 25–28 minutes, or until the pastry edges are nicely browned. Leave to cool before serving.

PEACH, LIME & PISTACHIO POLENTA CAKE

3 peaches

3 large eggs

200g caster sugar

3 unwaxed limes

150g fine polenta

175g pistachio nuts, finely blitzed in a food processor or mini chopper

150g salted butter, melted and cooled slightly, plus extra for greasing

FOR THE TOPPING

1 peach

150ml Greek yogurt

25g pistachio nuts, roughly chopped

2 tablespoons clear honey

Put the 3 peaches into a small saucepan, cover with boiling water and simmer for about 25 minutes, or until soft. Drain, then immediately plunge the peaches into cold water to cool them. Remove the stones, drain any excess water, then blitz the flesh in a blender until smooth.

Preheat the oven to 180°C (160°C fan), Gas Mark 4. Grease a 23cm springform cake tin and line it with baking paper.

Beat the eggs and sugar together in a bowl. Finely grate the zest of 2½ of the limes directly into the bowl. Add the polenta and blitzed pistachios, then mix well. Stir in the cooled melted butter and, lastly, the peach purée. Pour the mixture into the prepared cake tin and bake for 45–50 minutes, or until a skewer inserted into the centre of the cake comes out clean. Leave the cake to cool completely in the tin or overnight.

Remove the cake from the tin and place it on a serving plate. Prepare the topping just before you are ready to serve. Spread the Greek yogurt straight from the refrigerator over the surface of the cake. Alternatively if you're not going to eat the whole cake in one sitting you can slice the cake into portions and top each slice individually – see Tip.

Slice the peach and arrange on top of the yogurt. Scatter over the pistachios and finely grate the zest of the remaining lime half over the top. Drizzle over the honey and serve immediately.

TIP

Leftover cake refrigerates incredibly well covered in clingfilm, but bring it to room temperature to serve. You can always add the yogurt and topping to individual slices just before serving.

MINT TEA MOJITO

MAKES 4

1 large bunch (about 45g) of mint

8 teaspoons light brown sugar

200ml boiling water

2 English Breakfast tea bags

4 unwaxed limes, halved and each half cut
   into 6 segments

200ml dark rum

ice cubes

Pick 6 large mint leaves per glass and put them into 4 tumblers or highball glasses. Add 2 teaspoons of the sugar to each glass.

Pour the 200ml of boiling water into a teapot or heatproof jug. Add mint sprigs and the tea bags and infuse for 3–4 minutes. Stir well and remove the tea bags but leave the mint in. Leave to cool.

Distribute the lime segments among the glasses. Using either a mojito muddler or the end of a wooden spoon handle, crush the mint leaves, sugar and lime pieces in each glass, extracting as much juice from the limes as possible. Pour 50ml of the dark rum into each glass.

If the mint tea is cool (throw a few ice cubes in to cool it if necessary), add 50ml of the tea to each glass. Add ice cubes and stir, then serve.

QUICK FIX
FEASTS

I'm fairly certain when it comes to cooking a midweek dinner that the same thought often crosses our minds: 'Should I cook tonight? Or would it be easier to just order a takeaway?' I used to ask myself this question, and then I started to think 'OK, so if I order a takeaway, it takes 45 minutes, there are two of us and there is no way it's coming in at less than £30 and it might not even be that great.'

The truth is that sometimes we've just had a hectic day and are just too hard-pushed to cook a decent meal, and so convenience kicks in, whether shop-bought or dialled for... and that's OK, because that's real life. But to those of you who don't believe it's possible to make something delicious in a short amount of time, using few ingredients, I want to say that it is possible. I promise you, this is how I cook virtually all the time at home.

Once in a while, I may make a labour-intensive recipe, if I know the results are truly worth it, but for an average, everyday midweek dinner, I know that if I have a few basic ingredients (let's say, a bit of cheese in the fridge, some vegetables or cupboard staples like pasta, beans or rice, combined with stuff from my spice rack and, if I'm lucky, some element of fresh produce – whether meat, dairy, vegetables or fruit) I can whip up something perfectly decent. And not only can I do this in less time than it takes to get a takeaway, but the chances are that it will taste better and be more satisfying.

In this chapter I have put together some of my favourite dishes for quick-turnaround meals and also included a few side dishes that would suitably accompany any meal when you might need an additional element to bulk out a midweek feast. There is lots of flavour in these dishes but, in essence, the recipes are simple. Some are lighter, some need no cooking and some are a complete meal all-in-one, but all are delicious and genuinely useful for those times when life takes over and you just want to cook, eat and relax as quickly as possible.

QUICK-FIX FEASTS

MENU

Roasted cod loins with wild thyme & pul biber (see page 76)

Cumin-fried Padrón peppers with sumac, lemon & breadcrumbs (see page 85)

Burrata & burnt oranges with pistachios, mint & pomegranate (see page 87)

Spicy halloumi salad with tomatoes & fried bread (see page 88)

Accompaniment:
Toasted pitta bread

ULTIMATE CHICKEN SHAWARMAS

SERVES 2-8

600g boneless, skinless chicken thigh fillets
1 teaspoon ground turmeric
1 teaspoon ground cinnamon
1 teaspoon ground coriander
1 teaspoon ground cumin
1 teaspoon cayenne pepper
4 fat garlic cloves, crushed
finely grated zest of 1 unwaxed lemon
juice of ½ lemon
4 tablespoons Greek yogurt
olive oil
Maldon sea salt flakes and freshly ground black pepper

TO SERVE

6-8 round flatbreads of your choosing (or use pittas)
200g Greek yogurt
4 large tomatoes, sliced, then each slice cut in half
1 large red onion, halved and finely sliced into half-moons
1 small bunch (about 30g) of fresh coriander, roughly chopped
gherkins or cucumbers in brine (as many as you like), finely sliced

Place the chicken thigh fillets in a bowl. Add the spices, garlic, lemon zest and juice, yogurt, a good drizzle of olive oil (about 2 tablespoons) and a generous amount of salt and black pepper. Using your hands, work the marinade into the chicken, ensuring it is mixed evenly and coats every exposed part of all the fillets. Cover the bowl with clingfilm and marinate for at least 30 minutes or overnight in the refrigerator.

Drizzle a little olive oil into a large frying pan set over a medium heat. When the oil is hot, add the chicken – reduce the heat if the thighs begin to cook too quickly. Fry gently for 10–12 minutes on each side, or until the thighs have a nice, deep golden brown crust and are cooked through. When done, remove and cut the thighs widthways very thinly.

To serve, lay a flatbread on your work surface. Spread Greek yogurt across the surface. Place a line of tomato half-moons down the middle. Stack some shredded chicken over this, then follow with the onion, coriander and a few slices of pickled cucumbers. Fold up the bottom of the flatbread, then fold over the sides to enclose the filling as tightly as possible. Repeat with the remaining flatbreads and filling. To make eating the shawarmas a little easier, wrap the base with some doubled-up baking paper or a square of kitchen foil, to hold the juices in.

HARISSA SKIRT STEAK SANDWICHES

with sweet red onion pickle

SERVES 6-8

1kg skirt steaks

4 tablespoons rose harissa

vegetable oil

1–2 baguettes (depending on how much
bread you like)

2 handfuls of mixed salad leaves

Maldon sea salt flakes and freshly ground
black pepper

FOR THE SWEET RED ONION PICKLE

2 red onions, halved and thinly sliced into
half-moons

4 tablespoons rice wine vinegar (or use red
or white wine vinegar)

2 teaspoons pul biber chilli flakes

2 teaspoons nigella seeds

½ small packet (about 15g) dill,
roughly chopped

3 tablespoons caster sugar or golden
caster sugar

Coat the steaks well in the rose harissa, using your hands to really work the spice into the meat. When evenly coated on both sides, lay out the steaks, stacked on top of each other, on a plate and cover with clingfilm. Leave to marinate for 20 minutes.

Combine all the ingredients for the onion pickle in a bowl and mix well, ensuring the pickle dressing has evenly coated all the onions. Set aside.

Drizzle a little oil into a large, heavy-based frying pan and set it over a medium-high heat. When the oil is hot, place as much steak into the pan as you can fry in one go without overcrowding. Cook according to your liking – the length of time depends on the thickness of the steak. The best way to check is to test its firmness by poking the fattest part with your finger; if it is still very bouncy, it will be very rare. The firmer it becomes, the more well done the meat is. Ideally, you want something lovely and pinkish red on the inside so the cut is at its peak – juicy, tender and cooked to perfection. I find with most skirt steaks that 4–5 minutes cooking on each side over a medium-high heat does the trick. Transfer the cooked steak to a plate, cover with kitchen foil and leave to rest for 5 minutes as you continue cooking subsequent batches.

Once rested, slice the steak widthways into thin, juicy slivers. Season well with salt and pepper. Pile the slices into as much or as little bread as you like. Stir the pickle once more, then serve with the pickle spooned over the meat and some mixed salad leaves on top.

ROASTED COD LOINS

with wild thyme & pul biber

SERVES 4

4 cod loins (about 200g each), thicker
    pieces work best
garlic oil
4 teaspoons dried wild thyme
2 teaspoons pul biber chilli flakes
finely grated zest of 2 unwaxed lemons
Maldon sea salt flakes and freshly ground
    black pepper

Preheat the oven to 220°C (200°C fan), Gas Mark 7. Line a roasting tray with baking paper.

Place the fish fillets on to the prepared roasting tray and drizzle generously with garlic oil to coat each piece of fish. Sprinkle over the wild thyme, pul biber, lemon zest and a generous amount of salt and pepper.

Roast for 8–12 minutes depending on the thickness of your fish, or until the fish is cooked through. Serve immediately.

EASTERN PRAWN LINGUINE

with feta, garlic, pul biber & Greek basil

SERVES 4–6

olive oil

6 fat garlic cloves, bashed and thinly sliced

500g linguine

600g raw, peeled prawns

50g unsalted butter

finely grated zest of 2 unwaxed lemons

2–3 tablespoons pul biber chilli flakes

400g feta cheese, broken into rough
   1cm chunks

several handfuls of Greek basil leaves

Maldon sea salt flakes and freshly ground
   black pepper

Drizzle a generous amount of oil into a large frying pan set over a medium heat. When the oil is hot, add the garlic slivers and cook for about 2 minutes, or until they are translucent and soft – take care not to let them brown. Remove the pan from the heat and set it aside to allow the garlic to infuse the oil.

Cook the pasta according to the packet instructions. Drain the pasta, reserving a couple of ladlefuls of boiling liquid, and return the pasta to the pan.

Put the frying pan with the garlic slivers back on to the hob, add the prawns and fry them over a medium-high heat for a few minutes on each side, or until they are pink, opaque and completely cooked through.

Tip the contents of the frying pan into the cooked pasta. Add the butter and the reserved pasta cooking liquid and season generously with salt and pepper. Add the lemon zest and pul biber and stir well, then add the feta and Greek basil. Toss well and serve with an extra drizzle of olive oil.

CHICORY & PEAR SALAD

with sriracha honey dressing

SERVES 4–6

350–400g chicory, leaves separated

2 pears (any variety), sliced into very
   fine discs

75g pistachio nuts

FOR THE DRESSING

4 tablespoons sriracha sauce

2 tablespoons clear honey, plus extra to taste

juice of ½ lemon

2 tablespoons olive oil

Maldon sea salt flakes and freshly ground
   black pepper

Put the chicory leaves into a large bowl and add the pear slices
and pistachios.

Using a small whisk or fork, mix the dressing ingredients
together in a cup. Adjust the sweetness by adding extra honey
if desired, then pour the dressing over the salad, toss well and
serve immediately.

BLACK-EYED BEAN SALAD

with diced peppers, spring onions, dill & parsley

SERVES 4–6

2x 400g cans black-eyed beans

1 red pepper, cored, deseeded and finely diced

1 green pepper, cored, deseeded and
   finely diced

5 spring onions, thinly sliced from root to tip

1 small bunch (about 30g) of dill, finely
   chopped

1 small bunch (about 30g) of flat leaf parsley,
   finely chopped

2 celery sticks, cut lengthways into 3, then
   diced

3 tablespoons red wine vinegar

4 tablespoons olive oil

Maldon sea salt flakes and freshly ground
   black pepper

Combine all the ingredients in a large bowl and mix well.
Leave to rest for 20 minutes, then mix again, taste and adjust
the seasoning if desired, then serve.

SPICY CHICKPEA, HARISSA & CHEDDAR PITTAS

MAKES 10

1 teaspoon cumin seeds

1 teaspoon coriander seeds

olive oil

1 onion, finely chopped

3 fat garlic cloves, crushed

400g can chickpeas, drained

1 teaspoon ground turmeric

½ teaspoon ground cinnamon

finely grated zest of 1 unwaxed lemon

juice of ½ lemon

1 small bunch (about 30g) of fresh
coriander, finely chopped

Maldon sea salt flakes and freshly ground
black pepper

TO SERVE

1 heaped tablespoon rose harissa

10 mini pitta breads

150g mature Cheddar cheese, coarsely
grated

Heat a large frying pan over a medium-high heat, add the cumin and coriander seeds and dry-toast for about 1 minute, shaking the pan until they release their aroma and begin to brown a little, taking care not to let them burn. Crush the toasted seeds with a pestle and mortar. Set aside.

Return the frying pan to the hob. Add a good drizzle of olive oil and the onion and fry for 6–8 minutes, or until translucent and the edges start to brown. Add the garlic, crushed cumin and coriander mixture, chickpeas, turmeric and cinnamon and mix well. As you stir, lightly mash some (but not all) of the chickpeas to create texture. Now add the lemon zest and juice and season generously with salt and pepper. Mix well, then remove the pan from the heat. Stir in the coriander, reserving a little to garnish, and set aside.

Put the rose harissa into a bowl and stir in a drizzle of olive oil to loosen the consistency a little.

Lightly toast the pittas, just to warm them through. Slice open each pitta and spoon the chickpeas inside. Top with a little of the harissa mixture, some grated cheese and a little of the reserved fresh coriander to finish. Serve immediately.

CUMIN-FRIED PADRÓN PEPPERS

with sumac, lemon & breadcrumbs

SERVES 4–6

2 tablespoons cumin seeds

garlic oil

300g Padrón peppers

2 handfuls of fine, dried, natural breadcrumbs (not golden)

1 tablespoon sumac

finely grated zest of 1 unwaxed lemon

Maldon sea salt flakes

Heat a large frying pan or saucepan over a high heat and have a lid or splatter guard to hand. Tip in the cumin seeds, then add a generous amount of garlic oil to coat the base of the pan. Follow immediately with the Padrón peppers and stir-fry for 2 minutes, ensuring they are coated in the cumin seeds and oil. Cover the pan with a lid – you will hear the cumin seeds pop. At this point, shake the pan gently to toss the peppers, holding the lid on tightly. The peppers will start to shrivel, and after about 1 minute the skins will brown and blister. When this happens, transfer the peppers to a board or serving platter and season with a generous amount of sea salt flakes (do not crush the flakes – just scatter them over).

Return the pan to the hob, add the breadcrumbs and fry over a medium-high heat for 30–40 seconds, or until golden brown and crispy. Scatter the breadcrumbs over the peppers, followed by the sumac and lemon zest, then serve immediately.

BURRATA & BURNT ORANGES

with pistachios, mint & pomegranate

SERVES 2–4

1 orange or blood orange
extra virgin olive oil
200g ball of burrata
60g pomegranate seeds
25g pistachio nuts, roughly chopped
2 pinches of nigella seeds
½ teaspoon sumac
handful of mint leaves, torn
Maldon sea salt flakes and freshly ground
    black pepper

To segment the orange, use a small, sharp knife to cut away the top and bottom of the fruit. Rest the orange on the cut surface, then slice away strips of peel and pith to expose the flesh all around the orange. When peeled, slice out segments of orange and discard the leftover skin.

You can use 1 of 2 methods to burn the orange segments: either using a cook's blowtorch – blacken the slices on both sides or, alternatively, heat a frying pan on the highest heat available until hot, brush a little oil on to the orange segments on both sides and place them in the pan. Leave them to cook for 1 minute on each side, or until starting to blacken.

Place the ball of burrata in the centre of a serving plate and either leave it whole or (if you're like me) pull it apart into rough quarters (roughly scoring the top makes this easier to do). Arrange the burnt orange segments on the plate and scatter over the pomegranate seeds, pistachios, nigella seeds and sumac. Drizzle generously with olive oil, season with salt and pepper, scatter over the torn mint leaves and serve.

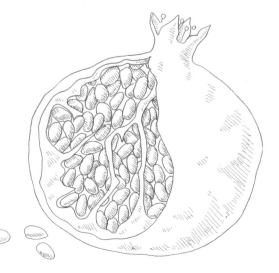

SPICY HALLOUMI SALAD

with tomatoes & fried bread

SERVES 4–6

600g tomatoes, cut into rough chunks

1 large red onion, finely sliced

1 large cucumber, halved lengthways, halved again and cut into 2.5cm dice

2 tablespoons dried oregano

finely grated zest and juice of 1 unwaxed lemon

olive oil

2 heaped teaspoons cumin seeds

2 heaped teaspoons coriander seeds

2 teaspoons black mustard seeds

1 heaped teaspoon chilli flakes, plus extra to taste

1 teaspoon Maldon sea salt flakes, plus extra to season

garlic oil (optional)

4–5 thick slices of sourdough bread or similar, preferably stale or left out to dry, cubed

2 x 250g blocks of halloumi cheese, each cut into 5 slices

freshly ground black pepper

1 small bunch (about 30g) of mint, leaves stripped, rolled up tightly and cut into thin ribbons, to garnish

Put the tomatoes, onion and cucumber chunks into a large mixing bowl. Add the oregano, lemon zest and juice and a good drizzle of olive oil, season well with salt and pepper and mix well. Set aside.

Heat a large frying pan over a medium-high heat, add the cumin seeds, coriander seeds, mustard seeds and chilli flakes and dry-toast for about 1 minute, shaking the pan until they release their aroma and begin to brown a little, taking care not to let them burn. Transfer to a mortar and add the sea salt flakes. Using a pestle, crush the seeds lightly to break them down just a little – you want to keep a lot of the texture. Add the crushed seed mix to the salad and mix well.

Line a plate with a double layer of kitchen paper. Set the same frying pan in which you toasted the seeds over a medium-high heat and drizzle in some olive or garlic oil. Once the oil is hot, add the bread pieces and fry on both sides for 4–5 minutes, or until deep golden. Transfer to the paper-lined plate and set aside.

Drizzle a little olive oil into the same pan, add the halloumi slices and fry for 1–2 minutes on each side, or until golden brown.

Add the fried bread to the salad and toss well to coat the bread chunks in the dressing. Adjust the seasoning as necessary, then arrange the salad and halloumi on a large platter and sprinkle with mint ribbons just before serving.

ROASTED APRICOTS

with ricotta, honey & pistachio crunch

SERVES 6

2 handfuls of fine, dried, natural
  breadcrumbs (not golden)

50g pistachio nuts, blitzed in a food processor
  or mini chopper or finely chopped

6–9 apricots (1 large apricot or 1½ small
  apricots per serving)

250g ricotta cheese

clear honey, for drizzling

freshly ground black pepper

Preheat the oven to the very highest temperature. Line a baking tray with baking paper.

Heat a large frying pan over a medium-high heat. Add the breadcrumbs and dry-toast for 6 minutes, then add the pistachios and dry-fry for about 1–2 minutes, or until the mixture is crunchy and golden. Remove from the heat and set aside.

Carefully halve and pit the apricots, then season with a good grinding of black pepper. Lay them on the prepared baking tray with their cut sides facing upward. They do not need any oil or other fat. Roast the apricots for 10 minutes, or until the edges are burnished and the fruit is slightly softened. Leave to cool.

Spoon a neat little spoonful or quenelle of ricotta on top of each apricot half, then drizzle over some honey. Scatter over the pistachio and breadcrumb 'crunch', then serve.

RASPBERRY, CARDAMOM & VANILLA YOGURT FOOL

SERVES 6–8

400g fresh raspberries

2 teaspoons vanilla bean paste

seeds from 5 cardamom pods, crushed using a pestle and mortar

300ml double cream

1–3 tablespoons icing sugar (depending on the sweetness of the fruit)

500ml thick Greek yogurt

Reserve 6–8 of the raspberries for decoration.

Using a food processor, blitz the remaining raspberries with the vanilla bean paste and crushed cardamom seeds until smooth.

Using an electric hand whisk, whisk the double cream and icing sugar together until stiff peaks form, then gently fold in the yogurt, one-third at a time. When all the yogurt is incorporated, gently fold in half the raspberry sauce, ensuring you fold (rather than stir) it in, to keep as much air in the mixture as possible. When incorporated, fold in the remaining raspberry sauce.

Divide the mixture among 6–8 glasses or dessert bowls. Place a raspberry on top of each serving. Refrigerate for at least 2 hours to firm up, or serve immediately if you can't wait.

TIP

I sometimes like to serve these with shortbread biscuits on the side.

VEGETARIAN FEASTS

The culinary world has evolved so much in the past 20 years that being vegetarian no longer means you need to suffer the limitations of bland, ill-thought-out dishes. And while many of us love a mushroom risotto or a nut roast, food has moved on. Personally, I've always felt the flavours and techniques of Middle Eastern cooking are incredibly well suited to vegetarians and vegans.

I have many vegetarian friends and can empathize with the lack of love that goes in to creating dishes to accommodate them at times. Since I became a chef and needed to create inspiring vegetarian dishes, I have embraced vegetables more than ever before. While I may not be a vegetarian, I have found that there are plenty of ways to create satisfying meals using vegetables that will please everyone around the table. A humble root vegetable can be brought to life with a little sprinkle of spice and just a couple more ingredients. Coming up with a vegetarian feast (not just a collection of recipes that feel like side dishes) can be easy if you combine a few straightforward ingredients from the kitchen cupboard with some fresh produce. You can create something not only abundant, colourful and simple but also – and most importantly – utterly satisfying.

More and more people are adding meat-free days to their weekly diets and there is absolutely no need for this to be a bland and tasteless affair. It's not complicated to create vegetarian dishes that will satisfy vegetarians and meat-eaters alike. For the carnivores among you, I am confident that you will find the following recipes in this chapter filling and satisfying (and likewise, vegetarians – there are plenty more meat-free recipes throughout this book) to keep your table filled with delicious dishes. And you don't need to label this as vegetarian cuisine because, really, it's just hearty, delicious, satisfying food. That's the best kind of food, I'm sure you'll agree.

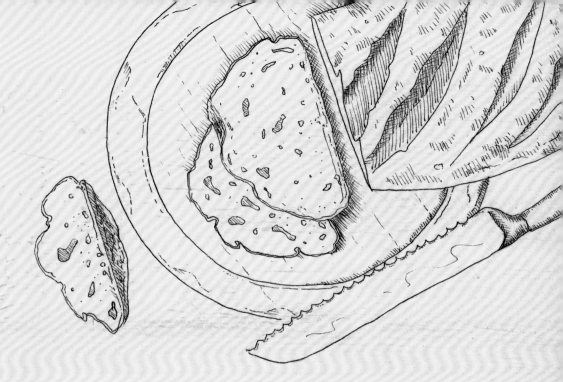

VEGETARIAN FEASTS

MENU

Polenta chips with cumin, garlic & feta (see page 100)

Quinoa patties with pomegranate molasses & yogurt (see page 103)

Carrot, orange, ginger & walnut dip (see page 104)

Green couscous & roasted veg with black garlic & preserved lemons (see page 109)

Sticky, spicy aubergines with toasted sesame seeds & spring onions (see page 110)

Spiced green bean & tomato stew with labneh, harissa oil & scorched peanuts (see page 113)

Accompaniments:
Harissa yogurt; toasted ciabatta

POLENTA CHIPS

with cumin, garlic & feta

MAKES 20

1 heaped teaspoon cumin seeds

275g polenta

4–5 fat garlic cloves, crushed

finely grated zest of 1 large unwaxed lime

500ml boiling water

1 teaspoon chilli flakes (optional)

1 small bunch (about 30g) of fresh
    coriander, finely chopped

200g feta cheese, crumbled

vegetable oil

2 eggs, beaten

Maldon sea salt flakes and freshly ground
    black pepper

Heat a large frying pan over a medium-high heat, add the cumin seeds and dry-toast for about 1 minute, shaking the pan until they release their aroma and begin to brown a little, taking care not to let them burn. Add 200g of the polenta, the garlic, lime zest, salt, pepper and the boiling water and stir vigorously to ensure the polenta breaks up and is a smooth, even consistency without lumps. Do not be tempted to add more water as this will make the chips impossible to fry. Transfer the cooked polenta to a plate, spread it out and leave to cool.

When cooled, put the cooked polenta into a mixing bowl and add the chilli flakes, if using, coriander and crumbled feta. Mix well until the ingredients are evenly incorporated.

Lay a sheet of greaseproof paper on a tray. Divide the mixture into 2 equal portions and spread out each portion into a long rectangular shape roughly 25 x 10cm and about 2.5cm thick. (Don't get too caught up with exact measurements – this is just a guideline.) Cut each block into 10 fingers, then put in the freezer for 1 hour to firm up.

Pour enough oil into a large saucepan or deep frying pan to deep-fry the polenta chips and heat over a medium-high heat. Line a plate with a double layer of kitchen paper. Prepare 2 shallow dishes, one with the beaten eggs and one with the remaining polenta.

When the oil is hot, remove the polenta chips from the freezer. Coat each finger all over, first in the eggs, then in polenta. Carefully lower the chips into the hot oil and fry for 2 minutes on each side, until crisp and golden. Remove with a metal slotted spoon and transfer to the paper-lined plate to drain the excess oil, then serve.

QUINOA PATTIES

with pomegranate molasses & yogurt

MAKES 16–18

200g quinoa

1 large egg

1 onion, very finely chopped

2 heaped teaspoons turmeric

2 heaped teaspoons ground cumin

1 heaped teaspoon ground cinnamon

100g ready-to-eat dried apricots, finely chopped (raisins or dried cranberries also work well)

1 small bunch (about 30g) of fresh coriander, finely chopped

4 tablespoons vegetable oil, plus extra if needed

Maldon sea salt flakes and freshly ground black pepper

TO SERVE

200g Greek yogurt

150g pomegranate molasses

Maldon sea salt flakes and freshly ground black pepper

Cook the quinoa for a little longer than the packet instructions (about 10–12 minutes), or until it is quite soft and swollen. Drain and rinse very well under cold running water to remove the starch and ensure all the quinoa is well rinsed and not stuck together. Shake well, then leave to drain.

Put the quinoa, egg, onion, spices, apricots and chopped coriander (reserving 1 tablespoon for garnish) into a large mixing bowl, season with salt and pepper and blend together. Squeeze the mixture with your hands so it sticks together. Shape the mixture into golf ball-sized balls, then pat them down to form nice, equal-sized patties – don't worry about making them too perfect, but ensure they are no thicker than 2cm.

Heat the oil in a large frying pan over a medium-high heat. Line a plate with a double layer of kitchen paper. Add the patties to the pan (in batches if necessary to avoid overcrowding the pan) and fry for 4–5 minutes on each side, or until deep golden brown. If necessary, add a little extra oil as they cook in order to get a nice crunchy base on each patty. Transfer the cooked patties to the paper-lined plate and leave to drain any excess oil.

Put the yogurt into a jug and season with salt and pepper. Stir in just enough water to thin the yogurt to the consistency of double cream.

Serve the patties with a generous amount of seasoned yogurt drizzled over, followed by the pomegranate molasses and a scattering of the reserved fresh coriander.

CARROT, ORANGE, GINGER & WALNUT DIP

SERVES 6–8

500g carrots, peeled and cut into 3 pieces

150g walnut pieces

1 small bunch (about 30g) of fresh coriander, finely chopped

1 heaped teaspoon ground cinnamon

½ teaspoon ground cloves

10cm piece of fresh root ginger, peeled and finely grated

2–3 fat garlic cloves, crushed

2 tablespoons clear honey

zest and juice of 2 unwaxed oranges

extra virgin olive oil

3 tablespoons nigella seeds

Maldon sea salt flakes and freshly ground black pepper

Cook the carrots in boiling water for 10 minutes, or until cooked through. Drain, then immediately plunge the carrots into cold water to arrest the cooking process.

Using a food processor, combine the walnuts (reserving a few for garnish), carrots, coriander (reserving some for garnish), spices, ginger, garlic, honey and orange zest and juice along with a generous glug (about 4 tablespoons) of olive oil. Blitz the mixture to a coarsely textured purée. Season with salt and pepper to taste. Drizzle in a little more olive oil to loosen the consistency if desired. Lastly, stir through the nigella seeds and serve with extra coriander and a few reserved walnut pieces arranged on top.

ROASTED PORTOBELLO MUSHROOMS

with pine nuts & halloumi

SERVES 4 AS A STARTER OR SIDE

4 large Portobello mushrooms

50g unsalted butter, softened

2 fat garlic cloves, crushed

1 small bunch (about 30g) of fresh coriander, very finely chopped

125g halloumi cheese, coarsely grated

2–3 tablespoons pine nuts, finely chopped

olive oil

Maldon sea salt flakes and freshly ground black pepper

Preheat the oven to 220°C (200°C fan), Gas Mark 7. Line a large baking tray with baking paper.

Arrange the mushrooms on the prepared tray with their gills facing upwards.

Combine the butter, garlic, coriander, halloumi and pine nuts in a bowl and season well. Drizzle in just a little olive oil and mix well. Divide the mixture into 4 portions and pile 1 portion into the centre of each mushroom, pressing it into the base.

Roast for 35–40 minutes, or until nicely browned, then serve.

ROASTED BEETROOT SALAD

with burnt chestnuts, tahini yogurt & herb oil

SERVES 4

1.5kg beetroot, roasted and peeled (or use vacuum-packed beetroot in natural juices), quartered

200g vacuum-packed cooked and peeled chestnuts

Maldon sea salt flakes and freshly ground black pepper

FOR THE YOGURT SAUCE
3 tablespoons tahini
100g Greek-style yogurt
2–3 tablespoons olive oil
1–2 tablespoons warm water

FOR THE HERB OIL
½ small bunch (about 15g) of dill
½ small bunch (about 15g) of fresh coriander
a good squeeze of lemon juice
finely grated zest of 1 unwaxed lemon
5 tablespoons olive oil, plus extra as needed

TO GARNISH
toasted sesame seeds
toasted nigella seeds

Arrange the beetroot quarters in a large platter.

Heat a large saucepan over a high heat. Put the chestnuts into the pan without oil and scorch them a little, about 2 minutes on each side, or until they are slightly blackened. Remove the chestnuts from the heat and arrange them on the platter with the beetroot.

To make the herb oil, pour a little boiling water into a bowl and immerse the dill and coriander in it. Leave to blanch for 1 minute, then drain and cool the herbs under cold running water.

Using a stick blender or mini chopper, blitz the herbs with a squeeze of lemon juice, the lemon zest, olive oil and some salt and pepper. Blend to a smooth mixture, adding more oil to loosen the consistency as necessary. Adjust the seasoning to taste and set aside.

Combine the ingredients for the yogurt sauce, adding just enough of the warm water to give the mixture a smooth sauce consistency. Drizzle the yogurt sauce over the beetroot. Spoon over the herb oil, then sprinkle with toasted sesame seeds and nigella seeds to garnish.

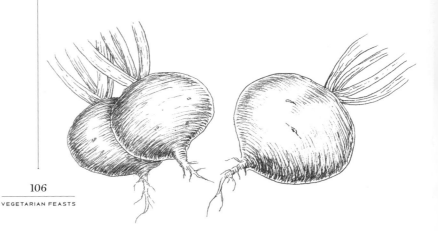

GREEN COUSCOUS & ROASTED VEG

with black garlic & preserved lemons

SERVES 6–8

2 courgettes, halved lengthways and sliced into 1cm thick half moons

1 red pepper, cored, deseeded and cut into 2.5cm squares

1 yellow or green pepper, cored, deseeded and cut into 2.5cm squares

2 red onions, halved and sliced into 1cm-thick half-moons

olive oil

300g couscous

6–8 preserved lemons, thinly sliced into rounds

1 head of black garlic, cloves thinly sliced

Maldon sea salt flakes and freshly ground black pepper

FOR THE HERB OIL

50g flat leaf parsley, leaves and stems roughly chopped

1 large bunch (about 50g) of fresh coriander, roughly chopped

olive oil

Preheat the oven to its highest temperature. Line a large baking tray with baking paper.

Put the courgettes, peppers and onions into the baking tray. Drizzle with a good amount of olive oil and season with salt and pepper. Use your hands to coat all the pieces in seasoned oil, then spread them out across the tray. Roast for 15 minutes, or until nicely brown, as desired.

Prepare the couscous according to the packet instructions, then fluff with a fork.

To prepare the herb oil, use a mini food processor or stick blender to blitz the parsley and coriander with enough olive oil to give the mixture a smooth herb oil consistency (a few tablespoons will do the trick). Season heavily with salt (as this salt will season the entire quantity of couscous) and, using a fork, stir the herb oil through the couscous until it is evenly combined. Lastly, stir in the roasted vegetables, preserved lemons and black garlic. Serve hot or at room temperature.

STICKY, SPICY AUBERGINES

with toasted sesame seeds & spring onions

SERVES 4–6 AS A SIDE

vegetable oil

3 large or 4 medium aubergines, halved lengthways and cut into 2.5cm-thick half-moons

about 2 heaped tablespoons rose harissa, plus extra as desired

4 tablespoons clear honey, plus extra as desired

Maldon sea salt flakes and freshly ground black pepper

TO GARNISH

2 teaspoons sesame seeds, lightly dry-toasted

1 teaspoon nigella seeds

½ small bunch (about 15g) of fresh coriander, leaves roughly chopped

4 spring onions, thinly sliced from root to tip

Heat a large saucepan over a high heat and add enough oil to fill 1cm up the side. Line a plate with a double layer of kitchen paper. Add the aubergines to the pan and coat them in the hot oil. The aubergines are like sponges and will immediately absorb the oil but, once cooked through, they will release some oil again. Fry the aubergines for 10–12 minutes, adding more oil as necessary to help them cook and tossing them every few minutes, or until they begin to shrink, soften and take on an even golden brown colour on all sides. Using a metal slotted spoon, transfer to the paper-lined plate. Lay a further 2 sheets of kitchen paper over the aubergine pieces to absorb excess oil.

Use kitchen paper to wipe any remaining oil from the frying pan. Transfer the aubergines back into the pan and add the harissa, honey and a generous amount of salt and pepper. Stir well until the aubergine pieces are evenly coated in the mixture. Adjust the levels of honey, harissa and seasoning as desired. Serve with the sesame seeds, nigella seeds, coriander and spring onions scattered over.

SPICED GREEN BEAN & TOMATO STEW

with labneh, harissa oil & scorched peanuts

SERVES 4–6

olive oil

1 large head of garlic, cloves bashed and
thinly sliced

400g trimmed green beans

2 teaspoons ground cumin

1 heaped teaspoon ground cinnamon

1 heaped teaspoon ground turmeric

400g tomatoes, cored and diced into
rough chunks

400g can chopped tomatoes

1 heaped teaspoon caster sugar

Maldon sea salt flakes and freshly ground
black pepper

TO SERVE

1 heaped tablespoon rose harissa

olive oil

200g labneh

2 generous handfuls of peanuts,
dry-toasted until slightly scorched

Drizzle enough oil into a large saucepan to generously coat the base and heat over a medium heat. Heat the oil over medium heat. Add the garlic slivers and stir-fry for 1–2 minutes, or until they soften. Add the green beans and cook for 4–5 minutes, or until they just begin to lose their rawness – they will deepen in colour to a more vibrant green and soften somewhat.

Stir the spices and fresh tomatoes into the saucepan, then increase the heat and add the canned tomatoes, sugar and a generous amount of salt and pepper. Simmer for 20 minutes, stirring occasionally, until the beans are well cooked and the sauce has somewhat reduced. Adjust the seasoning if desired.

Put the harissa into a jug and mix in enough olive oil to thin it to a slightly runny consistency.

Serve warm on a platter or in a shallow bowl, dotted with dollops of labneh and harissa oil and scattered with the scorched peanuts.

GARLIC, FENUGREEK
& CUMIN FLATBREADS

SERVES 4

250g wholemeal flour, plus extra
for dusting

2 large pinches of Maldon sea salt flakes,
crushed

1 teaspoon red chilli flakes (optional)

3 tablespoons dried fenugreek leaves

2 fat garlic cloves, crushed

ghee or olive oil

175ml lukewarm water, plus extra
as needed

6 pinches (about 1½ teaspoons) of
cumin seeds

melted butter, to serve (optional)

Put the flour into a large mixing bowl and make a well in the centre. Put the crushed salt, chilli flakes, if using, fenugreek, garlic, 1 tablespoon of the olive oil and the lukewarm water into the well. Mix with a fork, incorporating the flour into the wet mixture, until a dough begins to form. If the mixture is too wet, add more flour to bring it together; if it is too dry, mix in a little more lukewarm water to bring the mixture to a good dough consistency. Knead for 5 minutes. Leave to rest for 10 minutes, then knead once again for 2 minutes.

Dust your work surface with flour. Divide the dough into 6 equal balls and roll out each ball into a rough circle. Sprinkle each with a pinch of cumin seeds and press them into the dough.

Fold the circles in half and in half again. Roll out the folded dough gently into 15cm circles, applying very little pressure to your rolling pin – too much compression prevents the light layers from puffing up during cooking. Pour ½ teaspoon of the olive oil into a frying pan set over a medium heat. When the oil is hot, fry 1 of the dough circles for about 1 minute, or until the underside is golden in patches, then turn it over and fry for a further 1 minute, or until golden.

Stack the cooked flatbreads between layers of baking paper while you repeat with the remaining dough circles, using ½ teaspoon of oil each time to fry them. Serve brushed with melted butter or extra ghee if desired.

SPICED RHUBARB
& ALMOND CAKE

SERVES 8-10

400g rhubarb, trimmed and cut into
    5mm-thick slices

225g caster sugar, plus 2 tablespoons

3 teaspoons ground cinnamon

3 large eggs

2 teaspoons vanilla bean paste

2 teaspoons ground ginger

225g self-raising flour

150g salted butter, melted, plus extra
    for greasing

150g flaked almonds, 75g toasted

FOR THE FILLING

300ml double cream, cold from the fridge

seeds from 4 cardamom pods, crushed
    using a pestle and mortar

1 teaspoon ground cinnamon

2–3 tablespoons icing sugar

1 teaspoon vanilla bean paste

175g smooth blackberry jam

Preheat the oven to 160°C (140°C fan), Gas Mark 3. Grease a 24cm spring-form cake tin and line it with baking paper.

Put the rhubarb slices into a mixing bowl with the 2 tablespoons caster sugar and 1 teaspoon of the cinnamon and mix well. Set aside.

Put the eggs, remaining caster sugar, vanilla paste, remaining cinnamon and ginger into a large mixing bowl and beat together to mix thoroughly. Add the flour and melted butter and mix well, then mix in the rhubarb pieces, followed by the toasted flaked almonds. Give everything a thoroughly good mix to ensure the ingredients are evenly combined.

Pour the mixture into the prepared cake tin and use a spatula to smooth out the surface. Scatter the raw flaked almonds liberally over the top. Bake for 1 hour, or until a skewer inserted into the centre comes out clean. Leave to cool in the tin. Remove the cooled cake from the tin and cut it in half horizontally to make 2 sandwich layers. Use the layer covered in almonds as the top cake layer.

To make the cream filling, put the double cream into a mixing bowl with the cardamom, cinnamon, icing sugar and vanilla paste and beat using an electric hand whisk until soft peaks form and it just holds its shape. If you have time, refrigerate the cream to chill it before using. Spread the cream over the lower half of the cake. Stir the jam to loosen and spoon it over the cream, then sandwich with the top cake layer.

BANANA, COFFEE &
CHOCOLATE CHUNK CAKE

with salted caramel & peanut butter sundae top

SERVES 10–12

3 large eggs

3 very ripe large bananas, mashed to a fine
    purée

150g caster sugar

2 teaspoons vanilla bean paste

1 heaped teaspoon ground cinnamon

2 x 25ml shots of espresso, cooled

200g plain flour

100g ground almonds

1 teaspoon baking powder

200ml olive oil, plus extra for greasing

100g dark chocolate chunks

FOR THE TOPPING

340g smooth or crunchy peanut butter,
    at room temperature

200g salted caramel spread

100g dark chocolate, shaved or coarsely
    grated

handful of chopped nuts (optional)

Preheat the oven to 180°C (160°C fan), Gas Mark 4. Select a rectangular cake tin measuring approximately 34 x 23cm. Grease the tin and line it with baking paper.

Beat the eggs, bananas and sugar together, then add the vanilla paste, cinnamon and coffee and blend until the mixture is evenly combined. Add the flour, almonds, baking powder and olive oil and mix well, then stir in the chocolate chunks. When the mixture is smooth, pour it into the prepared cake tin and bake for 45–55 minutes, or until the sponge is golden on top and a skewer inserted into the centre of the cake comes out clean. Leave to cool in the tin.

Spread the peanut butter across the surface of the cooled cake. Drizzle over the salted caramel, then cover with the grated chocolate. Refrigerate for 1 hour. Once chilled, sprinkle over the chopped nuts, if using. To serve, remove the cake from the tin and cut into slices. I sometimes like to add squirty cream on top, too.

SUMMER
FEASTS

Living in England does mean I spend much of the year longing to feel the warmth of the sun on my face and waiting for the abundance of summer produce to come into play. The joy of sweet-tasting fruits, fresh green vegetables and the sizzling smoke of grilling and barbecuing with friends is the definition of summer in my mind.

We're not so fortunate in England to always have perfect summer weather, but the produce is still plentiful and, overall, we tend to entertain and be entertained more often during the summer months than in any other season. Drinks in hand, we come together to feast on colourful salads, delights from the barbecue both savoury and sweet, and plenty of delicious dishes perfect for sharing with a crowd.

I must confess, I don't have a garden, and therefore do not own a barbecue, so I tend to create summer recipes that you can make indoors, rain or shine, which to me evoke the true meaning of summer. You can really play with flavours during the warmer months, because there is an abundance of fresh ingredients to add wonderful little lifts to simple recipes. Everything from herbs, chillies, citrus zests and even fresh fruits come into their own and deliver the kind of flavour that satisfies everyone.

Summer dishes should be simple, colourful, feed many and satisfy everyone. This chapter reflects what I love to cook and eat most during summertime. (Although to be honest, produce permitting, some of these recipes work beautifully all year round.) Even if the sun is playing hide and seek with you, you can create dishes that deliver that summer vibe, no matter what the temperature outside may be.

SUMMER FEASTS

MENU

Blackened spatchcock chicken (see page 130)

Grilled corn in harissa mayo with feta, mint, coriander & chilli (see page 132)

Tamarind & honey pork ribs (see page 133)

Vine-baked sea bass with coconut, turmeric, lime, chilli & coriander (see page 137)

Orzo & tomato salad with capers & Kalamata olives (see page 142)

Accompaniment:
Toasted pitta bread or wraps

BUTTERFLIED LEG OF LAMB

with pomegranate salsa

SERVES 4–6

1kg butterflied leg of lamb

2 tablespoons natural yogurt

2 fat garlic cloves, crushed

2 tablespoons sun-dried tomato paste

1 heaped tablespoon finely chopped thyme

2 tablespoons lightly crushed coriander
 seeds

2 tablespoons olive oil, plus extra for
 cooking

Maldon sea salt flakes and freshly ground
 black pepper

FOR THE POMEGRANATE SALSA

200g pomegranate seeds

½ cucumber, finely diced (to the same size
 as the pomegranate seeds)

1 small red onion, very finely diced

1 teaspoon nigella seeds

8 large mint leaves, finely chopped

2 tablespoons pomegranate molasses

1 tablespoon olive oil

Remove the lamb from the refrigerator 20 minutes before you intend to marinate it and ensure it is splayed open and as flat as possible, so that the meat cooks evenly. If there are any sides with much thicker meat, use a small knife to make incisions to open them up and flatten these sides as evenly as possible.

Combine the remaining ingredients in a bowl to make a marinade, seasoning generously with salt and pepper. Rub the marinade all over the butterflied lamb leg and really work it in. Cover with clingfilm and marinate for a minimum of 30 minutes at room temperature, or overnight in the refrigerator, if preferred.

Preheat the oven to 220°C (200°C fan), Gas Mark 7. Line a baking tray with baking paper.

Drizzle a little olive oil into a large frying pan set over a medium heat. When the oil is hot, place the marinated lamb in the pan with the skin side facing down. Seal the lamb on all sides until nice and brown, without letting it blacken or burn. It should have a nice crust in about 10 minutes. Transfer the lamb to the prepared baking tray and roast for 15–20 minutes, depending on how you like your meat cooked. I like it very pink and juicy, but if you prefer medium or well done, leave it in for a further 5–10 minutes.

Meanwhile, combine all the ingredients for the salsa in a bowl, stir well and set aside.

Leave the lamb to rest, covered with kitchen foil, for 10 minutes before carving. Serve with the salsa.

SPICE-MARINATED BEEF KEBABS

SERVES 6–8

1kg beef bolar (or any cheap cut suited
  to quick cooking that your butcher
  recommends), cut into 4cm dice

1 teaspoon sweet smoked paprika (pimento)

1 teaspoon ground turmeric

2 teaspoons ground cumin

1 teaspoon ground cinnamon

3 garlic cloves, crushed

juice of ½ lemon

4–5 tablespoons olive oil, plus extra as
  needed

Maldon sea salt flakes and freshly ground
  black pepper

TO SERVE

sliced red onion

natural yogurt

fresh coriander

pitta bread or wraps

Note that this economical cut of beef is a little tougher than higher end cuts and therefore is best served medium-rare. If you prefer your beef medium or well done, I would suggest using either rump or sirloin steak instead.

Put the beef into a large mixing bowl, add the spices, garlic, lemon juice, a generous amount of salt and pepper and the oil, adding more if necessary to enable the spices to coat the beef pieces. Marinate at room temperature for 1 hour.

I find it easier and less messy to cook the beef pieces in a frying pan, then skewer them to serve. To cook, heat a large frying pan over a high heat. When the pan is hot, place some of the beef pieces in the pan, leaving just a little spacing between them, and cook for 2–3 minutes on each side, or until a deep brown crust forms. Transfer to a plate, cover with kitchen foil and leave to rest while you cook subsequent batches. Skewer the pieces of beef when ready to serve. Serve with onion slivers, yogurt and herbs in pitta breads or wraps.

BLACKENED SPATCHCOCK CHICKEN

SERVES 4

1.5kg chicken (ask your butcher to spatchcock it for you, if preferred)

1 tablespoon cumin seeds

2 teaspoons ground coriander

1 teaspoon ground cumin

seeds from 6 green cardamom pods, finely ground using a pestle and mortar

1 tablespoon pul biber chilli flakes

1 tablespoon dried thyme

grated zest of 1 unwaxed lemon

juice of ½ lemon

2 garlic cloves, crushed

1 heaped tablespoon caster sugar

3–4 tablespoons olive oil

Maldon sea salt flakes and freshly ground black pepper

If you prefer to spatchcock the chicken yourself, place the whole chicken, breastside facing down, on a chopping board and, using a sharp knife, make incisions on either side of the top of the spine. Insert the knife at an incision point and, carefully, using the spine as your guide, pull down the knife to cut away the spine from that side of the chicken. Repeat on the other side to release the spine and discard it (or use it for making stock). Now turn the bird over so that the breast side is facing upwards and press down firmly on it to flatten the carcass.

Combine the remaining ingredients in a bowl to make a spice paste, then rub it all over the skin side of the bird. Cover with clingfilm and leave to marinate for at least 20 minutes or overnight in the refrigerator.

Preheat the oven to 230°C (210°C fan), Gas Mark 8. Line a large baking tray with baking paper.

Lay the bird, with the skin side facing upwards, on the prepared baking tray. Roast for about 45 minutes, or until the chicken is cooked through and the skin is crisp and browned. Leave to rest for 10 minutes before serving. (This also works well on a barbecue. Position the chicken over indirect heat and cook for approximately 45 minutes.)

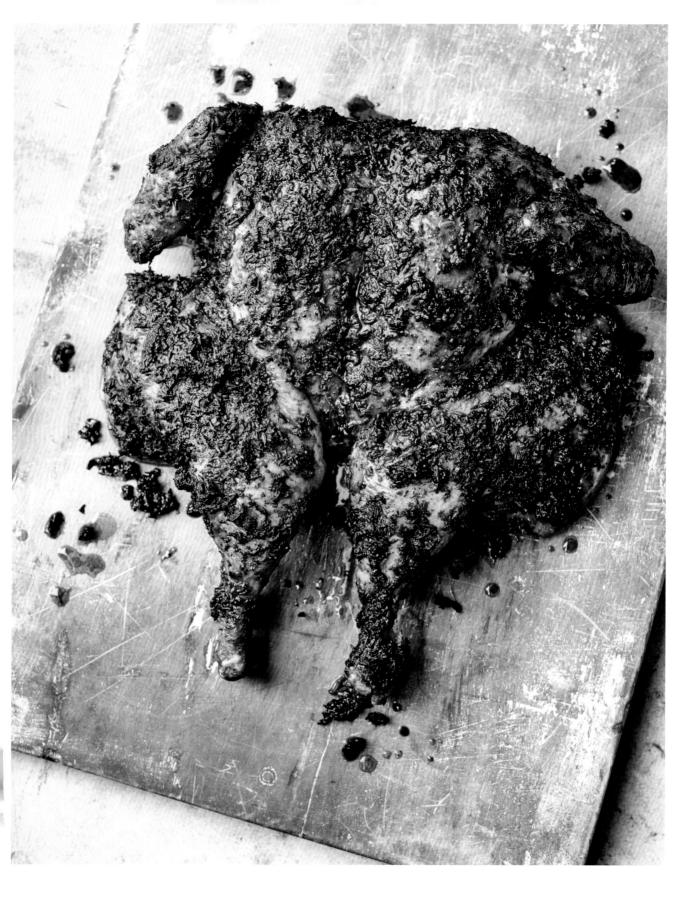

GRILLED CORN IN HARISSA MAYO

with feta, mint, coriander & chilli

MAKES 4

4 corn on the cobs
200g feta cheese, very finely crumbled
1 teaspoon chilli flakes
handful of finely chopped fresh coriander
6–8 large mint leaves, roughly chopped

FOR THE HARISSA MAYO
3 tablespoons mayonnaise
1 tablespoon rose harissa
finely grated zest of 1 lime
squeeze of lime juice
Maldon sea salt flakes and freshly ground
   black pepper

Combine the ingredients for the harissa mayo in a bowl, stir well and set aside.

Cook the corn in boiling water for 10 minutes. Meanwhile, heat a griddle pan over a medium-high heat. When the cooking time has elapsed, drain the corn and pat it dry with kitchen paper.

Place the corn cobs on the hot griddle pan and immediately increase the heat to high. Cook for 6–8 minutes, turning occasionally, until char marks appear and the corn is blistering in parts.

Spread the feta crumbs on a plate. Divide the mayo into 4 portions and spread 1 portion all over each cob. Roll the coated cobs in the feta. Sprinkle over the chilli flakes, fresh coriander and mint. Serve immediately.

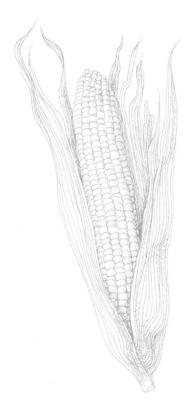

TAMARIND & HONEY PORK RIBS

SERVES 4–6

1.5kg pork ribs

75g tamarind paste

5 tablespoons clear honey

4 tablespoons tomato ketchup

3 fat garlic cloves, crushed

2 tablespoons dark soy sauce

1 tablespoon chilli flakes

2 teaspoons ground cinnamon

2 teaspoons ground cumin

finely grated zest and juice of 1 orange

Maldon sea salt flakes and freshly ground
   black pepper

Cook the ribs in gently simmering water for 45 minutes. Drain, then leave to cool completely. Put the cooled ribs into a shallow roasting tray or dish.

Put the remaining ingredients into a bowl and season generously. Pour the marinade over the ribs, ensuring it coats them entirely. You can cook them straight away, but ideally marinate in the fridge for a few hours, or overnight to allow the marinade to permeate the meat.

Preheat the oven to 190°C (170°C fan), Gas Mark 5. Line a large baking tray with kitchen foil.

Shake off any excess marinade from the ribs and spread them out on the prepared tray. Roast for 15 minutes, then baste with the marinade and roast for a further 15 minutes. Baste once again, increase the oven temperature to 200°C (180°C fan), Gas Mark 6 and cook for a further 10 minutes. Serve immediately.

VINE-BAKED SEA BASS

with coconut, turmeric, lime, chilli & coriander

SERVES 3-6

75g fresh coconut, finely grated

finely grated zest of 1 unwaxed lime

1 small bunch (about 30g) of fresh
    coriander, finely chopped

1 long red chilli, deseeded and very
    finely chopped

2 garlic cloves, bashed and crushed

10cm piece of fresh turmeric, finely grated

olive oil

30–36 vine leaves (allow 5–6 per fillet,
    depending on size), plus extra as required

6 sea bass fillets with skin on (about
    80–100g each)

Maldon sea salt flakes and freshly ground
    black pepper

Preheat the oven to 240°C (220°C fan), Gas Mark 9.
Line a large baking tray with baking paper.

Put the coconut, lime zest, coriander, chilli, garlic and turmeric
into a bowl and season generously with salt and pepper. Add a
little drizzle of olive oil and mix well to form a paste.

Using 5–6 barely overlapped vine leaves per fillet, make a sheet
of vine leaves on your work surface. Place a sea bass fillet on top
with the skin side facing downwards, as if you were wrapping a
present. Divide the topping mixture into 6 portions and spread
1 portion over the flesh of each fillet. Carefully wrap the fillets in
their vine leaf sheets, using extra leaves as necessary to ensure
the fish or topping is sealed well.

Transfer the wrapped fillets to the prepared baking tray and
roast for about 12 minutes, or until the fish is cooked through.
Serve immediately, unwrapping the parcels to serve.

POMEGRANATE, CUCUMBER & PISTACHIO YOGURT

SERVES 6–8

500ml thick Greek yogurt

1 large banana shallot or 2 small round shallots, finely chopped

1 large cucumber, cut into 1cm dice

150g pomegranate seeds, rinsed to remove any juice that may colour the yogurt

100g pistachio nuts

1 small bunch (about 30g) of mint, leave stripped and roughly chopped

olive oil

Maldon sea salt flakes and freshly ground black pepper

toasted pitta bread, to serve

Pour the yogurt into a large bowl and mix in the shallot. Add the cucumber, pomegranate seeds and pistachios (reserving a little of each for garnish). Add the mint, then fold the additions gently into the yogurt. Season generously with salt and pepper.

To serve, give the mixture a good drizzle of olive oil and scatter over the reserved cucumber, pomegranate seeds and pistachios. This yogurt is a great dip served with toasted pitta bread.

PEACH, FETA & MINT SALAD

with pul biber

SERVES 4–6

4 large peaches, pitted and each cut into approximately 10 wedges

1 red onion, thinly sliced into half-moons

extra virgin olive oil

1 tablespoon pul biber chilli flakes

juice of ½ lemon

200g feta cheese, crumbled into small pieces

1 small bunch (about 30g) of mint, leaves stripped, rolled up tightly and sliced into ribbons

Maldon sea salt flakes and freshly ground black pepper

Put the peach slices, onion, a good drizzle of olive oil, pul biber and lemon juice into a mixing bowl, season generously with salt and pepper and mix well.

Transfer the mixture to a serving dish, then scatter over the feta and mint and serve.

BROWN RICE SALAD

with olives, preserved lemons & apricots

SERVES 6–8

300g wholegrain (brown) basmati rice

400g can lentils

300g mixed olives, pitted and halved

1 bunch of spring onions, very thinly sliced from root to tip

250g dried apricots, cut into strips

1 large bunch (about 50g) of fresh coriander, roughly chopped

1 large bunch (about 50g) of flat leaf parsley, roughly chopped

2 tablespoons ground coriander

8 preserved lemons, deseeded and finely chopped

100g toasted flaked almonds

2 heaped tablespoons sumac

juice of 1 lemon

4 tablespoons clear honey

good drizzle of olive oil

Maldon sea salt flakes and freshly ground black pepper

Cook the rice according to the packet instructions, then drain and rinse in plenty of cold water to remove all the starch. Drain well in a sieve.

Combine the rice with the remaining ingredients and mix well to serve.

ORZO & TOMATO SALAD

with capers & Kalamata olives

SERVES 6–8

350g orzo pasta

2 x 290g deli packets of semi-dried/ sunblush tomatoes in oil, drained (reserve the oil) and cut into strips

400g green beans, trimmed and halved

200g pitted Kalamata olives (or 400g Kalamata olives, pitted), roughly halved

50g flat leaf parsley, leaves and stems finely chopped

400g feta cheese, crumbled into small chunks

100g pine nuts

240g capers in brine, drained

Maldon sea salt flakes and freshly ground black pepper

Cook the pasta according to the packet instructions. Rinse thoroughly in cold water and leave to drain for 10 minutes.

Transfer the drained pasta to a large mixing bowl. Add 2 tablespoons of the oil that was drained from the sunblush tomatoes and mix well to coat the pasta.

Cook the green beans in boiling water for 6–8 minutes, or until al dente, then plunge them into a bowl of cold water to arrest the cooking process. Drain well.

Add the cooled, drained green beans to the pasta with the remaining ingredients and mix well. Add a little more of the oil reserved from the sunblush tomatoes and season very generously with salt and pepper, then mix once more and serve.

BLUEBERRY, LIME &
GINGER CHEESECAKES

MAKES 4

10 ginger biscuits (such as Ginger Nuts – not the dark, thin ones), crushed

25g unsalted butter, melted

150g full-fat cream cheese

finely grated zest of 1 unwaxed lime, plus extra to decorate

150ml double cream

8 tablespoons blueberry jam, plus extra to serve (optional)

Put the biscuit crumbs into a small bowl and pour over the melted butter. Fork together until the crumbs have absorbed all the butter. Divide the mixture into 4 portions and spoon each of these into a martini glass or tumbler. Pat down gently to compress the crumbs and make a firm base for the cheesecakes. Transfer to the refrigerator.

Put the cream cheese, lime zest and double cream into a large mixing bowl and mix gently until the cream and cream cheese are just combined. Add the blueberry jam and gently stir it through the mixture so it is rippled with swirls of jam but not fully blended.

Remove the glasses from the refrigerator and divide the cheesecake mixture between them. Refrigerate for a minimum of 1 hour, or overnight, before serving. Decorate with lime zest and dollop on a little extra jam to serve if desired.

CHARGRILLED PINEAPPLE

with sweet lime & mint yogurt

SERVES 4

1 large pineapple
olive oil
4 tablespoons brown sugar

FOR THE YOGURT SAUCE
150g Greek-style yogurt
¾ small packet (about 20g) of mint, leaves
    stripped and finely chopped
finely grated zest of 1 unwaxed lime
good squeeze of lime juice
1 teaspoon icing sugar
1 tablespoon cold water, plus extra as
    required

TO DECORATE
1 long red chilli (not a small fiery one),
    deseeded and finely chopped
1 tablespoon brown sugar (optional)

Heat a griddle pan over a high heat.

If you prefer, leave the pineapple skin on and simply eat around it when cooked. Otherwise, to remove the skin, first cut off the stem using a large knife, then cut away a circular disc from the base and discard. Now cut away strips of the outer skin from top to bottom until all the skin is removed. Use a small knife to cut away any brown fibrous spots. Cut the pineapple into quarters lengthways. Cut away the tough core from each quarter.

Brush the cut sides of the pineapple with a little oil to prevent them from sticking. Coat 1 side of each wedge with ½ tablespoon of the brown sugar and place sugar-coated side down on the hot griddle pan. Griddle for 6–8 minutes without moving, or until char marks begin to appear. Brush the other sides with oil and coat with sugar, then griddle for a further 6–8 minutes, or until equally charred. Transfer the pineapple wedges to serving plates.

Combine the yogurt, mint (reserving a little to decorate), lime zest and juice and icing sugar in a bowl and mix until smooth. Add the measured cold water to loosen the consistency of the sauce to that of double cream, adding more cold water as necessary.

Drizzle the yogurt sauce over the pineapple and scatter over the chopped chillies, brown sugar, if using, and reserved mint and serve.

LIGHTER

FEASTS

Every now and then, I overindulge. We all do – it's part of the nature of juggling busy work and home lives. Sometimes when we're feeling down, a little indulgence can cheer us up, and when we're on the go, it can be quick and easy to grab things to eat that aren't terribly nutritious or energy-sustaining.

I'm not much of a diet guru so don't mistake this chapter for a low-calorie diet section. That's just not my style – I always say I enjoy cake and salad in equal measure. This is simply a collection of recipes that sums up the kind of food I like to eat when I want dishes that are satisfying and a little lighter, and perhaps don't require much else with them. Some dishes are more virtuous than others, the idea being that they are balanced and delicious, because that is the point really. I dislike the notion that lighter or healthier eating needs to rely on bland, flavour-free, overly simple food, and the misconception that it revolves solely around all that is green or sprouted.

I tend to be a balanced cook, especially when at home. I prefer to cook food with intense flavours, made with simple ingredients boosted with a little spice or citrus and fresh herbs. You'll find in this chapter some of my favourite lighter meals – recipes that are every bit as satisfying as you would expect a good meal to be. We all want dessert, but maybe we don't always want to go the whole hog and indulge in something too exuberant. Simplicity has its beauty and this chapter, in essence, is more to do with simplicity in content, not necessarily in flavour or process. Fresh flavours, and satisfying and enticing foods, whatever the weather… those are the ones we will most likely turn to, time and again.

LIGHTER FEASTS

MENU

Yogurt & harissa marinated chicken (see page 156)

Smoked mackerel & quinoa salad with charred asparagus
& cannellini beans (see page 159)

Aubergine rolls with goats' cheese, herbs & walnuts (see page 162)

Avocado, grapefruit & cashew salad with harissa vinaigrette (see page 167)

Pomegranate bulgur wheat salad with almonds, feta & sour cherries (see page 168)

Accompaniments:
Crusty bread; tomato salad

CHICKEN & TURMERIC VERMICELLI SOUP

SERVES 4–6

150g vermicelli rice noodles

7.5cm piece of fresh root ginger, peeled and cut into 3–4 slices

7.5cm piece of fresh turmeric, halved lengthways (or 1 teaspoon ground turmeric)

3 garlic cloves, crushed

1 tablespoon chilli flakes (optional)

2.25 litres cold water (or use fresh vegetable or chicken stock)

300g shredded cooked chicken (leftovers are ideal)

2 carrots, peeled, halved lengthways and sliced

3–4 handfuls of chopped kale, tough stalks discarded

4 spring onions, thinly sliced from root to tip

1 small bunch (about 30g) of mint, leaves stripped, rolled up tightly and sliced into ribbons

1 small bunch (about 30g) of fresh coriander, roughly chopped

Maldon sea salt flakes and freshly ground black pepper

Rinse the rice vermicelli under cold running water, then put it into a heatproof bowl and pour over enough boiling water to cover the noodles well. Leave to soak for 10 minutes, then drain the noodles and rinse them under cold running cold water. Set aside.

Put the ginger, turmeric, garlic and chilli, if using, into a large, deep saucepan set over a medium heat and pour in the measured water or stock. Season well with salt and pepper and give the mixture a stir, then add the chicken, bring the mixture to a simmer, reduce the heat to low and simmer gently for 30 minutes. If the soup simmers too aggressively, you may need to add more water and adjust the seasoning.

Remove and discard the fresh turmeric, then add the noodles, carrots and kale and cook for a further 5 minutes, or until the vegetables are tender. Check and adjust the seasoning as necessary. Remove the pan from the heat, stir in the spring onions, mint and coriander. Serve immediately.

TIP

You can use 350g raw peeled tiger prawns instead of the chicken – just add them with the noodles and ensure they are pink and cooked through before serving.

YOGURT & HARISSA
MARINATED CHICKEN

SERVES 4–6

6 largeish chicken breasts, butterflied
vegetable oil

FOR THE MARINADE
150ml thick Greek yogurt
**1 small bunch (about 30g) of fresh
   coriander, roughly chopped**
2 garlic cloves
2 tablespoons rose harissa
zest of 1 unwaxed lime
juice of ½ lime
1 tablespoon olive oil
**Maldon sea salt flakes and freshly ground
   black pepper**

Put the marinade ingredients into a food processor and season generously with salt and pepper. Blitz the mixture until smooth.

Put the butterflied chicken into a shallow dish. Pour the marinade over the chicken and leave to marinate for a minimum of 30 minutes or in the refrigerator overnight. If you have refrigerated the chicken, remove it from the refrigerator 20 minutes before cooking.

Drizzle enough vegetable oil into a large frying pan to just coat the base and set it over a medium heat. When the oil is hot, remove the chicken from the marinade, shake off any excess, then add the chicken to the pan. Fry for approximately 8 minutes, or until nicely browned and cooked through. Pile the chicken pieces on to a serving platter and serve hot.

SMOKED MACKEREL & QUINOA SALAD

with charred asparagus & cannellini beans

SERVES 6

350g red quinoa

250g asparagus tips

olive oil, for brushing

500g smoked mackerel fillets (either plain or peppered works well), flaked

400g can cannellini beans, drained

2 tablespoons pul biber chilli flakes

100g pumpkin seeds

Maldon sea salt flakes and freshly ground black pepper

FOR THE DRESSING

finely grated zest and juice of 1 orange

2 tablespoons red or white wine vinegar

1–2 teaspoons Dijon mustard

3–4 tablespoons extra virgin olive oil

Cook the quinoa according to the packet instructions. Rinse thoroughly under cold running water, then leave in a sieve to drain.

Put the asparagus tips into a heatproof bowl, pour over enough boiling water to cover them and leave to blanch for 5 minutes. Drain the asparagus, then plunge into a bowl of cold water. Leave to cool in the water, then pat dry with kitchen paper.

Heat a griddle pan over a high heat. Brush the cooled asparagus tips with a little olive oil and griddle them for about 2 minutes on each side, or until char marks appear. Cut each asparagus tip into 3 roughly equal pieces and set aside.

Put the quinoa into a large bowl. Add the mackerel, cannellini beans, asparagus, pul biber and pumpkin seeds and mix well.

Combine the dressing ingredients, season with salt and pepper and mix well. Pour the dressing over the salad and toss. Season well with salt and pepper and serve.

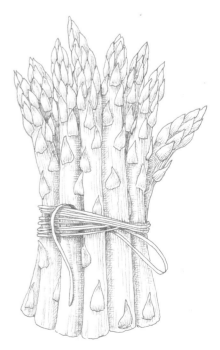

SMOKED SALMON

with capers, olives & preserved lemons

SERVES 4–6

500g smoked salmon

1 heaped teaspoon pul biber chilli flakes

75g nonpareille (tiny) capers

100g pitted mixed olives, sliced widthways

2 banana shallots, cut into wafer-thin rings

4 preserved lemons, deseeded, 4 roughly chopped and 2 thinly sliced into discs

3–4 tablespoons extra virgin olive oil

Maldon sea salt flakes and freshly ground black pepper

Swedish rye crispbreads, to serve

Lay the smoked salmon on a large, flat platter. Sprinkle over the pul biber, then scatter over the capers, olives, shallots and both the chopped and sliced preserved lemons. Drizzle lightly with olive oil and season with salt and pepper. Serve with Swedish rye crispbreads.

AUBERGINE ROLLS

with goats' cheese, herbs & walnuts

SERVES 4-6

3 large aubergines, cut lengthways into
    5mm slices
olive oil, for brushing
300g soft mild goats' cheese
1 small bunch (about 30g) of fresh
    coriander, finely chopped
1 small bunch (about 30g) of dill,
    finely chopped
150g walnuts, finely chopped
2 fat garlic cloves, crushed
1 heaped teaspoon ground fenugreek
½ teaspoon cayenne pepper
Maldon sea salt flakes and freshly ground
    black pepper

TO SERVE
150g Greek yogurt
100ml pomegranate molasses
150g pomegranate seeds

Heat a griddle pan over a medium-high heat. Line a plate with a double layer of kitchen paper. Brush each slice of aubergine with olive oil on both sides. When the griddle pan is hot, griddle the aubergines for about 6 minutes, or until grilled and cooked through. Transfer to the paper-lined plate to drain excess oil. Leave to cool.

Put the goats' cheese into a bowl and add the coriander and dill (reserving 1 teaspoon of each chopped herb for garnish). Add the walnuts, garlic, fenugreek and cayenne pepper and season generously with salt and pepper.

Place 1 tablespoon of the goats' cheese mixture on to the wider end of each cooled aubergine slice. If you have filling remaining, divide it among the slices equally. Roll up the aubergine slices around the filling and place the rolls on a tray or serving plate. At this point you can refrigerate the rolls so they set and hold their shapes – remove from the refrigerator 20 minutes before serving.

Put the yogurt into a bowl and stir in just enough water to give the yogurt the consistency of single cream. Drizzle the yogurt generously over the rolls, followed by the pomegranate molasses. Scatter over the pomegranate seeds and reserved herbs to serve.

SAUTÉED KALE SALAD

with pumpkin seeds, apple, feta & chilli sauce

SERVES 6–8

500g kale, tough stalks discarded, cut into bite-sized pieces

olive oil

4 Braeburn apples

juice of ½ lemon

extra virgin olive oil, for drizzling

200g feta cheese, crumbled

chilli sauce (such as sriracha)

50g pumpkin seeds

Maldon sea salt flakes and freshly ground black pepper

Wash the kale, but avoid shaking off all the water from the leaves – the kale will steam in this water later.

Drizzle enough olive oil into a large saucepan to just coat the base and set it over a medium–high heat. When the oil is hot, add the kale and season generously with salt and pepper. Stir-fry for 1 minute, or until just wilted. Cover the pan with a lid and steam the kale for 2 minutes, shaking the pan (with the lid on) a few times during cooking to keep the kale from sticking to the base of the pan. When the kale is cooked and turns a darker shade of green, transfer it to a bowl and leave to cool for a couple of minutes.

Chop the apple into thin strips and toss in the lemon juice.

Arrange the kale on a serving platter and drizzle over some extra virgin olive oil. Scatter the apple and feta over the kale, then drizzle over some chilli sauce to taste. Finish with a scattering of pumpkin seeds and serve.

AVOCADO, GRAPEFRUIT & CASHEW SALAD

with harissa vinaigrette

SERVES 4–6

100g rocket leaves

2 large red or pink grapefruit

2 large avocados

100g toasted cashew nuts

½ small bunch (about 10g) of chives, snipped into 5cm lengths

Maldon sea salt flakes and freshly ground black pepper

FOR THE HARISSA VINAIGRETTE

2 tablespoons rose harissa

2 tablespoons clear honey

1 tablespoon red or white wine vinegar

3 tablespoons olive oil

1 teaspoon water

Lay the rocket leaves across a serving platter.

To segment the grapefruit, use a small, sharp knife to cut away the top and bottom of the fruit. Rest the grapefruit on the cut surface, then slice away strips of rind to expose the flesh. When peeled, slice out segments of grapefruit and discard the leftover skin. Repeat with the other grapefruit. If large, slice the segments into half-moon slices.

Halve the avocados, remove the stones, peel the fruit, then cut each half into strips or chunks. Arrange the avocado and grapefruit over the rocket. Scatter over the cashew nuts and season generously with salt and pepper. Scatter over the chives.

Combine the harissa, honey, vinegar and oil in a small jug, then stir in about 1 teaspoon water to thin out the dressing a little. Season with salt and pepper. Drizzle the dressing over the salad and serve immediately.

POMEGRANATE BULGUR
WHEAT SALAD

with sour cherries, almonds & feta

SERVES 6–8

**800ml pomegranate juice
(100% pomegranate – I use Pom)**

200g bulgur wheat

1 tablespoon honey (optional)

olive oil

**1 small bunch (about 30g) of dill,
finely chopped**

**1 small bunch (about 30g) of flat leaf
parsley, finely chopped**

**2 long red chillies, deseeded and very
finely chopped**

100g flaked almonds

200g dried sour cherries (sweetened)

200g feta cheese, finely crumbled

**Maldon sea salt flakes and freshly ground
black pepper**

Put the pomegranate juice into a saucepan and bring to the boil over a medium heat. Add the bulgur wheat and simmer for 20–25 minutes, or until the juice is mostly absorbed by the grains. If you wish to offset the sharp flavour, add the honey while the bulgur wheat is cooking. Leave to cool.

Fluff the cooled bulgur grains with a fork. Drizzle over a little olive oil and season well with salt and pepper. Stir well, then add the chopped dill and parsley, chillies, flaked almonds and sour cherries, mixing them in with a fork to prevent them from sticking together. Lastly, add the feta and fork it through, then serve.

TIP

**Don't be put-off by the colour of the bulgar
wheat – different brands of pomegranate
juice will be different strengths of colour
– go by the flavour of the overall dish.**

WATERMELON, RADISH
& WATERCRESS SALAD

with pickled cucumber

SERVES 6–8

½ watermelon, balled using a melon baller

200g radishes, quartered or roughly chopped

100g watercress

nigella seeds, to garnish

FOR THE PICKLED CUCUMBER

1 cucumber

1 teaspoon caster sugar

3 tablespoons rice wine vinegar

Maldon sea salt flakes

FOR THE DRESSING

1½ tablespoons clear honey

½ teaspoon cayenne pepper

½ teaspoon ground cinnamon

olive oil

reserved cucumber pickling liquid (see method)

Maldon sea salt flakes and freshly ground black pepper

Halve the cucumber lengthways, then scoop out and discard the seeds. Cut the cucumber halves into thin slices. Put them into a large mixing bowl and season generously with salt. Add the sugar and rice wine vinegar. Using your hands, mix everything together, ensuring the cucumber slices are well coated in the mixture. Leave to stand for 15–20 minutes. Toss the cucumbers once again in the juice that has formed in the bowl, then drain the cucumbers, reserving 2 tablespoons of the liquid in a separate bowl. Set both aside.

To make the dressing, add the honey, cayenne pepper, cinnamon and a good drizzle of oil to the reserved cucumber pickling liquid and mix well.

Arrange the watermelon, radishes, watercress, and pickled cucumber slices on a serving platter. Scatter over some nigella seeds and serve with the dressing.

POMEGRANATE &
ROSEWATER JELLIES

MAKES 4

4 leaves of gelatine

450ml pomegranate juice (100 per cent
    pomegranate – I use Pom)

2 tablespoons alcohol-free rose water

75g caster sugar

100g pomegranate seeds

In a small bowl, soak the gelatine leaves in cold water for about 5 minutes, or until soft.

Meanwhile, set a small saucepan over a low heat and pour in the pomegranate juice and rose water. Stir in the sugar. Heat the mixture gently, just until the sugar dissolves, then immediately remove the pan from the heat.

Add the soaked gelatine leaves, 1 at a time, to the pomegranate juice mixture and stir until each leaf is dissolved before adding the next. Leave the mixture to cool for about 20 minutes, or until lukewarm.

Pour the liquid into 4 glasses or cups. Sprinkle the pomegranate seeds over each cup. Leave to cool completely, then refrigerate the jellies overnight or for a minimum of 4 hours before serving.

RASPBERRY & PISTACHIO
FROZEN YOGURT POTS

MAKES 6

150g fresh raspberries

1 teaspoon vanilla bean paste

300g Greek yogurt

75g pistachio nut slivers or chopped
    pistachio nuts

2 tablespoons clear honey

TO DECORATE

6 frozen raspberries

25g pistachio nut slivers

Using a blender, purée the raspberries, vanilla paste, yogurt, pistachios and honey together until smooth. Divide the mixture into 6 dessert cups or small bowls, then freeze overnight.

Remove the pots from the freezer 10 minutes before you want to serve them. Crumble over a frozen raspberry on top of each pot, then sprinkle over a few pistachio slivers just before serving.

SPECIAL OCCASIONS

In selecting a collection of recipes for all-important occasions, I wanted to place the emphasis on special-feeling dishes – recipes for times when you want to impress people or treat friends and loved ones to food with a little more thought and depth given to it than usual. These types of recipes usually signify a greater deal of effort that has gone into making them.

The following recipes are dishes that will make a menu feel celebratory. While there are a few dishes in this chapter that – although they may not be terribly complicated – may take some time to cook or prepare, there are also simpler dishes to help create perfect balance, not only in terms of menu creation but also time spent in the kitchen. I am particularly proud of the show-stopping Fig & Rose Millefeuille (see page 203), because it looks as though you've slaved away for hours, but it couldn't be simpler to prepare. The very last thing I want to do when I am cooking a special meal is to spend the entire time in the kitchen, missing out on the fun – the whole point of entertaining is to be with your loved ones.

Personally, I feel the most special occasions include convivial, simple and abundant food on the table, surrounded by the kind of people I can genuinely feel at ease with, even if they've all showed up dressed glamorously for the party while I only manage to make it to the table in a onesie, smelling of roasted meats and fried things... those are the best kind! With a little thought and some easy prep, you can achieve so much and I hope this chapter inspires you to host your own special occasions more often.

SPECIAL OCCASIONS

MENU

Griddled lobster tails with barberry, garlic, lime & chilli butter (see page 187)

Jumbo prawns with tomato, dill & fenugreek (see page 188)

Beer-roasted pork shoulder with plum sauce (see page 182)

Saffron roast potatoes (see page 190)

*'Confetti' rice with courgettes, aubergines, peppers,
pine nuts, sultanas & herbs (see page 197)*

Accompaniment:
Wilted chard or greens

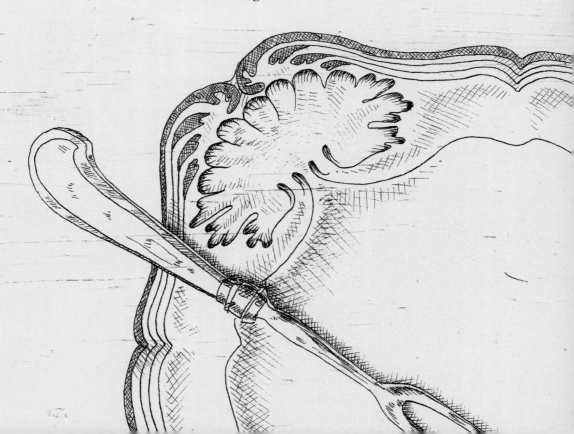

SPICED LAMB HOTPOT

SERVES 4–6

1 tablespoon cumin seeds

6 cardamom pods, lightly cracked

vegetable oil

2 large onions, thinly sliced into half-moons

900g diced leg of lamb

1 large garlic bulb, cloves peeled and left whole

8 shallots, peeled and left whole

2 large carrots, peeled and cut into 1cm dice

1 teaspoon ground cumin

1 teaspoon ground ginger

1 teaspoon ground cinnamon

½ teaspoon cayenne pepper

1 teaspoon English mustard powder

2 tablespoons plain flour

500ml chicken, lamb or vegetable stock

700–750g red potatoes, unpeeled, thinly sliced

50g unsalted butter, melted

sprinkling of thyme leaves

Maldon sea salt flakes and freshly ground black pepper

Preheat the oven to 170°C (150°C fan), Gas Mark 3½.

Heat a large flameproof casserole over a medium heat. When the pan is hot, add the cumin seeds and cardamom pods and dry-toast for about 2 minutes, stirring occasionally to prevent burning, until the spices release their aroma.

Pour enough oil into the pan to coat the base. When the oil is hot, add the onions and fry for 6–8 minutes, or until translucent and the edges start to brown. Add the meat and cook for a few minutes, stirring to coat in the oil and cumin seeds. Add the garlic cloves, shallots and carrots and stir for a couple of minutes, then add the ground cumin, ginger, cinnamon, cayenne pepper, mustard powder and flour and a generous seasoning of salt and pepper. Mix well, then stir in the stock.

Arrange the potato slices on top of the meat, slightly overlapping them. Brush with the melted butter, sprinkle with thyme leaves and season again with salt and pepper, then cover the casserole with a lid and transfer to the oven to cook for 1½ hours.

Take the hotpot out of the oven and remove the lid. Increase the oven temperature to 220°C (200°C fan), Gas Mark 7. Return the casserole to the oven, uncovered, and cook for a further 30–40 minutes, or until the potatoes are golden brown. Serve immediately.

BEER-ROASTED PORK SHOULDER

with plum sauce

1.5–2kg shoulder of pork

olive oil

4 teaspoons dried wild oregano
(or regular oregano)

3 teaspoons celery salt

3 teaspoons English mustard powder

3 teaspoons coarse black pepper

3 teaspoons ground coriander

650ml pale ale or lager

FOR THE PLUM SAUCE

600g plums, pitted and roughly chopped

3 teaspoons ground coriander

1 teaspoon cayenne pepper

½ small bunch (about 15g) tarragon,
leaves finely chopped

200ml water, plus extra as needed

Maldon sea salt flakes and freshly ground
black pepper

Preheat the oven to 170°C (150°C fan), Gas Mark 3½. Line a large roasting tin with baking paper.

Place the pork joint in the prepared tin and, if any string has been used to tie it together, remove it. Score the skin, then drizzle over some olive oil and rub it into the meat.

Mix the oregano, celery salt, mustard powder, pepper and coriander together in a small bowl. Scatter the mixture all over the pork and use your hands to rub it in, especially on the underside and deep into the skin on top. Pour the beer around the pork and add a little splash on top, ensuring you don't rinse off the spice mixture. Roast for 4 hours, or until cooked through – check the joint after 3 hours and if it is browning excessively, cover it with a double layer of kitchen foil for the remaining cooking time.

If the skin has not crisped up when the cooking time has elapsed, remove the pork from the oven and increase the oven temperature to 220°C (200°C fan), Gas Mark 7. Using tongs, carefully peel the skin off the meat and lay it flat on a rack over a baking tray. Roast the skin for a further 10–15 minutes, or until crispy. Meanwhile, cover the pork loosely with foil and leave to rest for about 30 minutes.

To make the sauce, put the plums, ground coriander and cayenne pepper into a saucepan set over a medium-low heat and season with salt and pepper. Sweat the plums for about 15 minutes, mashing them until they soften and are cooked. Stir in the chopped tarragon and add the water, increase the heat to medium and cook gently for about 10 minutes, or until the sauce has reduced to a gravy-like consistency. Add more water if necessary to reach your preferred sauce consistency.

Carve or shred your pork and serve with the crackling and plum sauce.

SPICE-ROASTED QUAIL

with sour cherry sauce

SERVES 4

½ teaspoon coarse black pepper

1 teaspoon ground cumin

½ teaspoon ground turmeric

pinch of ground cloves

olive oil

4 quails (approx. 150g each), giblets
  removed

25g salted butter, softened

FOR THE SOUR CHERRY SAUCE

100g dried sour cherries (sweetened),
  very finely chopped

½ teaspoon ground cinnamon

clear honey

Maldon sea salt flakes and freshly ground
  black pepper

Preheat the oven to 220°C (200°C fan), Gas Mark 7. Line a baking tray with baking paper.

Mix the dry spices together in a small bowl. Drizzle a little olive oil over each quail, then divide the dry spice mix between the quails, sprinkling it over. Use your hands to rub the spices into the oil and coat the birds all over, then place them on the prepared baking tray. Season generously with salt, then roast for 30–35 minutes.

Meanwhile make the sauce. Put the sour cherries into a small saucepan set over a medium-low heat, pour in just enough boiling water to cover them and bring to a gentle simmer. Add the cinnamon and cook for 6–8 minutes, or until the mixture has a sauce-like consistency, adding a little more water if needed. Season well with salt and pepper, and add a little honey to sweeten the sauce to your taste, then add the butter and stir until melted. When you're happy with the flavour, stir well and leave to simmer until the quails are cooked.

Remove the quails from the oven, cover loosely with kitchen foil and leave to rest for 6–8 minutes. Serve the quails whole or halved, with the sauce.

GRIDDLED LOBSTER TAILS

with barberry, garlic, lime & chilli butter

SERVES 4–8

75g salted butter, softened

finely grated zest of 1 unwaxed lime

2 tablespoons barberries, very finely chopped or blitzed in a food processor

2 garlic cloves, crushed

2 tablespoons finely chopped fresh coriander

1 heaped teaspoon chilli flakes

4 lobster tails (about 100g each), fresh or frozen (defrosted if frozen)

Maldon sea salt flakes and freshly ground black pepper

Combine the butter with the lime zest, barberries, garlic, coriander, chilli and a generous amount of salt and pepper until evenly blended. Refrigerate until needed.

Heat a griddle pan over a high heat.

Using a large, sharp knife, split each of the lobster tails in half lengthways. Place the split tails, with their shells facing downwards, on to the hot griddle pan – the shells will heat up and cook the lobster meat inside. Remove the flavoured butter from the refrigerator and dot two-thirds of it across the exposed lobster flesh. When it begins to melt, use a pastry brush to baste the lobster meat with it. Leave to cook for 2 minutes, then turn the lobster tails so that the flesh sides are facing downwards and cook for 45 seconds. Flip them over to check if the meat is opaque and cooked through. Dot the meat with the remaining butter and, when it begins to melt, transfer to a serving platter and serve immediately.

JUMBO PRAWNS

with tomato, dill & fenugreek

SERVES 4

olive oil

1 large onion, halved and thinly sliced into half-moons

3 fat garlic cloves, crushed

1 teaspoon ground turmeric

400g can chopped tomatoes

4 large tomatoes, each cut into 8 pieces

1 heaped tablespoon tomato purée

3 tablespoons (or 5 if frozen) dried fenugreek leaves

1 tablespoon fenugreek seeds, dry-toasted and ground to a powder using a pestle and mortar

1 teaspoon ground cinnamon

1 heaped teaspoon chilli flakes

1 teaspoon caster sugar

800g large raw prawns, or raw peeled prawns

25g salted butter

½ small bunch (about 15g) of dill, roughly chopped

Maldon sea salt flakes and freshly ground black pepper

toasted bread or rice, to serve

Drizzle enough oil into a large frying pan to just cover the base and set it over medium heat. When the oil is hot, add the onion and fry for 6–8 minutes, or until translucent and the edges start to brown.

Add the garlic to the pan and cook for 30 seconds, then add the turmeric and cook for a further minute. Next add the canned and fresh tomatoes, tomato purée, fenugreek leaves and ground fenugreek seeds, cinnamon, chilli and sugar and stir well to blend the spices into the sauce. Reduce the heat to low, season with salt and pepper, cover partially with a lid and simmer gently for about 30 minutes. Stir occasionally to prevent it from burning.

Heat a separate frying pan over a high heat. When the pan is hot, add the prawns and fry for 30–40 seconds on each side, to seal. Remove the prawns from the frying pan and stir them into the sauce to finish cooking. Add the butter and stir until incorporated, then remove the pan from the heat, stir in the dill (leaving some for garnish), scatter more dill on top and serve with bread or rice.

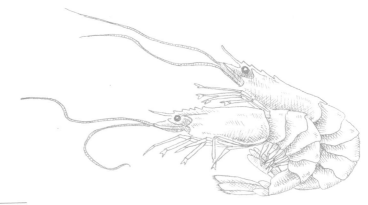

SAFFRON ROAST POTATOES

SERVES 4–6

1g Iranian saffron

2 generous pinches of Maldon sea salt flakes, plus extra to season

2–3 tablespoons boiling water

1.5kg Maris Piper or King Edward potatoes

2 tablespoons table salt

6 tablespoons vegetable oil or light olive oil

Preheat the oven to 190°C (170°C fan), Gas Mark 5. Line a large baking tray with baking paper. Line a plate with a double layer of kitchen paper.

Using a pestle and mortar, grind the saffron with the sea salt flakes to a fine powder. Add the boiling water and set aside to infuse.

Peel the potatoes, then trim any larger potatoes to ensure all the potatoes are of roughly the same size. Put them into a pan of cold water to rinse off the excess starch, then drain. Bring a large saucepan of water to the boil, add the table salt and parboil the potatoes for 8–10 minutes.

Drain the parboiled potatoes in a colander and leave to stand for 5 minutes to allow the excess moisture to evaporate. Shake the colander to help fluff up the potatoes and rough up the edges. Transfer the potatoes to the prepared baking tray.

Combine the saffron solution with the oil, mix well and pour the mixture over the potatoes. Season generously with sea salt flakes. Using a large metal spoon, turn the potatoes in the saffron oil to coat them. Season again, then roast for 30 minutes. Remove the tray from the oven, give it a good shake, then bake for a further 45 minutes, or until crispy. Transfer to the paper-lined plate to drain excess oil. Serve immediately.

CHARRED CAULIFLOWER

with tahini, harissa honey sauce & preserved lemons

SERVES 6

2 large cauliflowers

3 tablespoons rose harissa

4 tablespoons clear honey

1 tablespoon olive oil, plus extra for frying

1 teaspoon ground cinnamon

4 tablespoons light tahini

6 tablespoons Greek yogurt

good squeeze of lemon juice

Maldon sea salt flakes and freshly ground
  black pepper

TO SERVE

6 preserved lemons, deseeded and thinly
  sliced into rounds

generous handful of toasted flaked
  almonds

½ small bunch (about 15g) of flat leaf
  parsley, roughly chopped

Cut away any outer leaves from the cauliflowers, then cut each cauliflower into 4 slices of equal thickness. On the slices cut from the outer edges of the cauliflowers, trim and shave away enough of the curves to create flat surfaces, so that the slices cook evenly.

Combine the harissa, honey, olive oil and cinnamon in a small bowl, season with salt and pepper and mix well. Brush or rub the mixture over the cauliflower slices.

Drizzle a little oil into a large frying pan set over a medium heat. When the oil is hot, fry the cauliflower slices for 6–8 minutes on each side, or until they are cooked through and charred nicely on both sides. Blackening will occur as the spice paste is not only dark but also contains sugar (in the honey), which will burn naturally. This is part of the flavour of the dish and nothing to be worried about. (Alternatively, roast the cauliflower slices in a preheated oven, 220°C (200°C fan), Gas Mark 7, for 20–25 minutes.)

Meanwhile, mix the tahini with the yogurt and lemon juice in a bowl, season generously with salt, then stir in a little lukewarm water, 1 tablespoon at a time, until the mixture has a sauce-like consistency.

Transfer the cauliflower slices to serving plates. Drizzle over the yogurt sauce and any remaining marinade, then scatter over the preserved lemon slices, toasted almonds and parsley to serve.

TIP

To make this a vegan recipe, substitute coconut or soya yogurt for the Greek yogurt.

PAN-ROASTED PEPPERS

with a sweet harissa glaze

SERVES 6

1 tablespoon cumin seeds

olive oil

6 large peppers (I like to use a mix of red, yellow and orange), cut vertically into 7–8mm-thick strips

1 teaspoon ground cinnamon

2 tablespoons rose harissa

3–4 tablespoons clear honey

1 tablespoon red wine vinegar

½ small bunch (about 15g) of flat leaf parsley, roughly chopped, plus extra to garnish

Maldon sea salt flakes and freshly ground black pepper

Heat a large frying pan over a medium-high heat, add the cumin seeds and dry-toast for about 1 minute, shaking the pan until they release their aroma and begin to brown a little, taking care not to let them burn. Drizzle in enough oil to coat the base of the pan and increase the heat. Add the peppers and cook for 8–10 minutes, stirring occasionally, until they begin to soften and brown around the edges.

Add the cinnamon, harissa and honey to the pan and season generously with salt and pepper. Lastly, add the vinegar and stir to coat the peppers in the sauce. Cook for 2 minutes, then remove the pan from the heat, stir in the parsley and adjust the seasoning if desired. Scatter with chopped parsley and serve as a topping for bruschetta or as a condiment for cheese. They are also great alongside chorizo sausages.

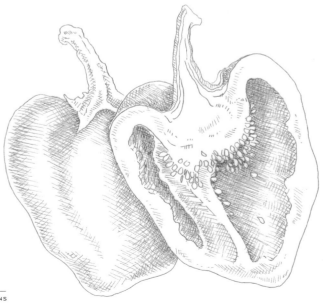

194

'CONFETTI' RICE

with courgettes, aubergines, peppers, pine nuts,
sultanas & herbs

SERVES 4–6

olive oil

1 large onion, very finely chopped

1 large aubergine, very finely diced

1 red pepper, very finely diced

1 green pepper, very finely diced

2 courgettes, very finely diced

100g sultanas

100g pine nuts

1 small bunch (about 30g) of dill, finely chopped

1 small bunch (about 30g) of flat leaf parsley, finely chopped

500g basmati rice

50g salted butter, cut into small pieces

Maldon sea salt flakes and freshly ground black pepper

Drizzle a generous amount of olive oil into a large frying pan set over a medium-high heat. When the oil is hot, add the onion and fry for 6–8 minutes, or until translucent and the edges start to brown. Add the aubergine and fry until it starts to turn golden, then add the peppers and courgettes and continue to fry for a further 1 minute. Remove the pan from the heat. Stir in the sultanas and pine nuts and season generously with salt and pepper. Stir in the herbs and set aside.

Cook the rice according to the packet instructions. Fluff the grains with a fork, then tip the rice into a large mixing bowl.

Stir the butter into the vegetable mixture. Pour the mixture over the rice. Using a large spoon, fold the vegetable 'confetti' through the rice without mashing or crushing the rice. Adjust the seasoning if needed and serve immediately.

TIP

When preparing the vegetables it is important to chop them all into very small dice and all the same size – this attention to detail will ensure the finished dish looks more refined.

BLACKBERRY & APPLE SANDWICHES

with rosemary & orange cream

MAKES 12

3 large eggs
225g golden caster sugar
1 tablespoon vanilla bean paste
2 teaspoons ground cinnamon
225g plain flour
2 teaspoons baking powder
225g salted butter, melted
1 large Braeburn apple, cut into 1cm dice
125g blackberries, halved

FOR THE ROSEMARY & ORANGE CREAM

1 heaped teaspoon rosemary leaves
3 tablespoons golden caster sugar
300ml double cream
finely grated zest of 1 unwaxed orange

Preheat the oven to 180°C (160°C fan), Gas Mark 4. Line a 12-hole muffin tin with paper muffin cases.

Put the eggs, sugar, vanilla paste and cinnamon into a large mixing bowl and beat together. Stir in the flour and baking powder, then add the melted butter and mix until smooth. Fold in the apple and blackberries – don't worry if you mash them slightly.

Divide the mixture between the muffin cases and bake for 40 minutes, or until the muffins are deep golden brown and a skewer inserted into the centres of the cakes comes out clean. When cooked, remove them from the tin and leave to cool.

To make the cream, blitz the rosemary leaves with the sugar in a spice grinder until the mixture turns into a fine dust. Transfer the mixture to a large bowl and add the cream and orange zest. Beat using an electric hand whisk until soft peaks form and it just holds its shape.

When the cakes are cool, remove them from the paper cases and slice them in half horizontally. Spread the cream over the lower half of each cake, then sandwich together with the top halves and serve.

CHERRY, DARK CHOCOLATE & MINT PARFAIT

SERVES 6

2 large eggs, separated

75g caster sugar

1 teaspoon vanilla bean paste

300ml double cream

½ small packet (about 15g) of mint, leaves stripped, rolled up tightly and roughly chopped

175g frozen pitted cherries, defrosted and roughly chopped (reserve any excess juices)

50g dark chocolate chunks

Line a 900g loaf tin with a double layer of clingfilm, leaving plenty of clingfilm overhanging the tin.

Put the egg yolks, sugar and vanilla paste into a large mixing bowl. Using an electric hand whisk, whisk the mixture until pale, thick and creamy.

In a separate bowl, whip the cream until soft peaks form, then gently whisk the cream into the egg mixture.

Wash the beaters on the electric whisk, then whisk the egg whites in another bowl until stiff peaks form. Gently fold the whisked egg whites through the egg mixture until evenly combined.

Add the mint, cherries (and any juice) and dark chocolate chunks to the bowl and carefully fold them into the mixture.

Transfer the mixture to the prepared loaf tin. Cover the parfait with the overhanging clingfilm and freeze for at least 6 hours, or overnight.

To serve, remove the parfait from the freezer and leave to soften for a few minutes. Unfold the clingfilm on top and use the edges to lift the parfait out of the tin. Flip it on to a serving tray or chopping board, discard the clingfilm and use a flat-bladed knife to smooth over the surface, dipping it into hot water occasionally to clean the knife and achieve a smooth finish. Leave to soften slightly for 10–15 minutes, then slice and serve immediately. This is great served with wafers, nuts and dark chocolate sauce, or sandwiched in brioche buns.

TIP

You can use fresh cherries for this dish instead of frozen – use roughly the same quantity of pitted cherries and soften them briefly in a pan with 1 heaped tablespoon caster sugar, then leave to cool.

FIG & ROSE MILLEFEUILLE

with pistachios & a passion fruit & honey cream

1 sheet of ready-rolled all-butter puff pastry

2 tablespoons caster sugar

600ml double cream

2–3 tablespoons clear honey,
plus extra to serve

pulp and seeds from 3 large or 4 small
passion fruits

½ small packet (about 15g) of mint, leaves
stripped, rolled up tightly and sliced
into ribbons

4–5 fat black figs, thinly sliced into about
5 slices

75g pistachio nut slivers or roughly chopped
pistachio nuts

3 tablespoons dried edible rose petals,
lightly ground using a pestle and mortar

Preheat the oven to 210°C (190°C fan), Gas mark 6½. Line a baking tray with baking paper.

Gently prick each side of the pastry about 20 times, working evenly and neatly across the sheet. Cut the pastry sheet into 3 equal-sized rectangles, then lay them on the prepared baking tray. You need to prevent them from rising more than 1cm, so place an inverted baking tray over them. Bake for 20 minutes, then remove the most attractive-looking rectangle (to use as the top layer) and leave to cool. Return the remaining pastry rectangles, covered with the inverted baking sheet, to the oven and bake for a further 7 minutes, or until deep golden brown and crisp. Leave to cool.

When the first rectangle removed from the oven is cool, brush the top with lukewarm water, then scatter over the sugar. Return to the oven to bake for 7 minutes, or until crisp and golden brown, and the top is nicely glazed. Leave to cool.

Whip the cream with the honey until nice and thick, then drizzle in the passion fruit seeds and stir gently to marble it through the cream, ensuring you don't fold it through completely.

To assemble, take a cooked pastry rectangle as your base and place it on a serving platter. Spread one-quarter of the cream on top. Scatter over one-third of the mint and arrange half the fig slices on top of the cream. Scatter over one-third of the pistachios. Spread another quarter of the cream on top of the pistachios, then sprinkle over one-third of the rose petal powder. Now place the second pastry rectangle on top and repeat the layering process. Place the sugar-crusted pastry lid on top, then scatter over the remaining mint, pistachios and rose petals. Give the millefeuille a final drizzle of honey and serve.

COMFORT
FOOD

Comfort food is often defined as warming, cheese-laden pasta-, potato-, rice- or bread-based dishes, or pies, casseroles and other hearty fare. I guess this entirely depends on the comforting moment you associate with that dish – the significant person who once made it for you, or maybe a warm holiday memory. However, comfort food can mean one thing to one person and something entirely different to another. Although I absolutely love cheesy, creamy, carb-heavy warming winter dishes, for me comfort food is usually anything that I can eat that makes me smile and allows me to be utterly comfortable while eating it!

I have a terrible habit of eating in bed. Not eating at bedtime but the physical act of eating in my bed. Since I started writing books, I spend an inordinate amount of time testing in my kitchen late into the night, so as a treat I really enjoy the luxury of reclining in bed, perhaps like a much less glamorous version of a Roman empress, holding a bowl or plate of food and enjoying it in the sanctuary of my own bed, and that to me is the ultimate comfort.

Comfort aside, the food itself has to be pretty spectacular. A salad of just leaves never really provides me with much comfort, it must be said, but add some shredded meat, feta, chillies, a little spice and some croutons and suddenly we are out of Saladville and into Comfort Town territory. Mostly, comfort food is bold in flavour, whether simple or complex, and requires no formality to enjoy. These are recipes that you can happily indulge in – or overindulge in – and you won't be sorry later, as they satisfy and give you a little of what you fancy. Because, as we all know, a little of what you fancy does you good.

COMFORT FOOD

MENU

Lamb kofta roll (see page 215)

Lamb, plum & preserved lemon stew (see page 219)

Spicy beef noodles with green beans (see page 220)

Cardamom & coconut dhal with turmeric & nigella seeds (see page 223)

Freekeh, tomato & chickpea pilaf (see page 227)

Accompaniments:
*Cooked basmati rice; natural yogurt with fresh mint;
radish & celery salad*

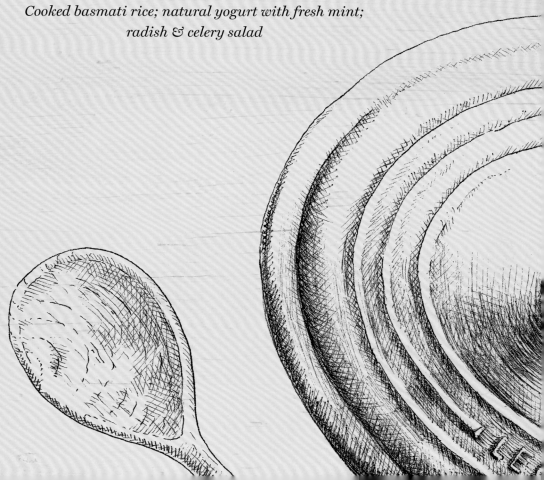

CAULIFLOWER, ANARI, BLACK PEPPER & THYME QUICHES

MAKES 12

1 cauliflower

olive oil

2 teaspoons freshly ground black pepper, plus extra to taste

handful of thyme leaves, finely chopped

400ml double cream

75g dry Anari cheese, finely grated

3 sheets of filo pastry

3 large eggs

Maldon sea salt flakes

Chop the cauliflower (florets and stem) into 1cm cubes and put them in a large frying pan set over a medium heat. Dry-fry for a couple of minutes to extract any excess moisture, stirring frequently. Drizzle in a little olive oil, continuously moving the cauliflower around the pan to avoid it browning. Add the pepper, chopped thyme and double cream and stir well. Just as the cream begins to bubble, remove the pan from the heat and stir in the grated cheese. Season the mixture with salt and pepper and leave to cool completely.

Preheat the oven to 200°C (180°C fan), Gas Mark 6. Brush the holes of a 12-hole muffin tin generously with olive oil.

Cut each filo pastry sheet into 8 squares, roughly about 12cm square. Overlap 1 pastry square with another to make an 8-pointed star. Push the stars into the holes of the muffin tin.

When the cauliflower mixture has cooled, mix in the eggs thoroughly. Distribute the mixture equally between the 12 pastry cases, then bake for 30 minutes, or until the tops are nicely golden and a skewer inserted into the centre of the quiches comes out clean. Serve warm.

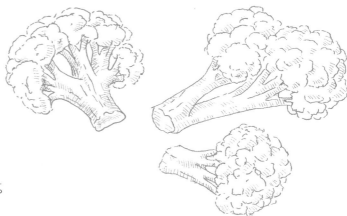

TIP

If you can't find Anari cheese, substitute feta or goats' cheese instead.

BLACK GARLIC, TAPENADE, & FETA ROLLS

MAKES 10–12

450g strong white bread flour, plus extra for dusting

7g sachet of fast-action dried yeast

1 teaspoon caster sugar

300ml warm water

2 tablespoons olive oil, plus extra for drizzling

150g black olive tapenade

2 heads of black garlic, cloves thinly sliced

2–3 tablespoons dried wild thyme

200g feta cheese, crumbled

Maldon sea salt flakes and freshly ground black pepper

Combine the flour, yeast and sugar in a large mixing bowl and crumble in 2–3 good pinches of sea salt flakes and a grinding of pepper. Pour 275ml of the water into the flour mixture, along with the olive oil, then bring the dough together first using a fork, then with your hands. If it feels dry, mix in just enough of the remaining water to just dampen it; otherwise, drizzle over a little olive oil to keep it moist.

Knead the dough for a couple of minutes, then leave to stand for 10 minutes. Knead it again for 1 minute. Repeat this process once more: knead the dough for 2 minutes, leave to stand for 10 minutes, then knead again for 1 minute. Put the dough into a clean bowl, cover the bowl with a clean tea towel and leave it somewhere warm to rise for about 1½ hours, or until it has almost doubled in size.

Line a baking tray with baking paper. Dust your work surface with flour.

Knock back the dough in the bowl, punching it a couple of times with your fist. Transfer the dough on to your floured surface and, using a rolling pin, roll it out into a rectangle measuring about 40 x 30cm. Spread the tapenade across the surface of the dough, then place the black garlic slices evenly across the tapenade. Scatter over the wild thyme and crumbled feta. Roll up the dough to make a long 40cm roll. Using a sharp knife, cut the roll into 10–12 slices.

Lay the slices on the prepared baking tray, ensuring there is 3cm between each slice to allow them to expand during cooking. Cover the tray loosely with clingfilm and leave to prove for 30 minutes, or until the slices have almost doubled in size.

Meanwhile, preheat the oven to 200°C (180°C fan), Gas Mark 6. When the rolls are ready, bake for 35–40 minutes, or until golden brown. Transfer to a wire rack and leave to cool before serving.

LAMB KOFTA ROLL

SERVES 4-6

500g minced lamb

3 eggs

1 small bunch (about 30g) of flat leaf parsley, finely chopped

2 tablespoons pul biber chilli flakes

4 fat garlic cloves, crushed

3 tablespoons tomato purée

1 onion, very finely chopped

1 sheet of ready rolled all-butter puff pastry

1 tablespoon nigella seeds

Maldon sea salt flakes and freshly ground black pepper

TO SERVE

150ml Greek yogurt

chilli sauce

Preheat the oven to 200°C (180°C fan), Gas Mark 6. Line a baking tray with baking paper.

Combine the meat with 2 of the eggs, the parsley, pul biber, garlic, tomato purée and onion in a large bowl. Season generously with salt and pepper. Mix the ingredients with your hands until the mixture becomes a smooth, evenly mixed paste.

Unroll the pastry. Lay the meat in a long sausage shape across the centre of the pastry. Fold the pastry over the sausage and pinch the pastry around the meat to seal it. Transfer to the prepared baking tray.

Beat the remaining egg and use it to brush the pastry all over. Sprinkle over the nigella seeds. Bake for about 25 minutes, or until the pastry is deeply golden brown and crispy.

Transfer the roll to a serving platter and slice to serve. Serve hot with yogurt and your favourite chilli sauce on the side.

PARSNIP & APPLE SOUP

SERVES 6-8

vegetable oil

2 onions, chopped

10cm piece of fresh root ginger, finely grated

3 teaspoons fennel seeds, dry-toasted and finely ground using a pestle and mortar

seeds from 6 green cardamom pods, finely ground using a pestle and mortar

1kg parsnips, peeled and cut into chunks

6 apples, peeled, cored and cut into chunks

2 litres vegetable stock

6 tablespoons horseradish cream

Maldon sea salt flakes and freshly ground black pepper

pumpkin seed oil, to garnish (optional)

Pour enough vegetable oil into a large saucepan to cover the base, add the onions and fry over a medium heat for 6–8 minutes, or until softened. Add the ginger, ground fennel and cardamom seeds and mix well, then stir in the parsnips and apples. Sweat for a few minutes without browning until the parsnips have softened.

Pour in the stock, then season with salt and pepper. Simmer for about 45 minutes, or until the parsnips can be easily mashed. Stir in the horseradish cream, then remove the pan from the heat and leave to cool until just warm. When cooled, use a stick blender to purée the soup to your preferred consistency.

Drizzle over a little pumpkin seed oil if desired, season with pepper and serve.

HARISSA-INFUSED
LEG OF LAMB

with fenugreek & lime

SERVES 4–6

2kg leg of lamb

FOR THE MARINADE
200g Greek yogurt
4 teaspoons fenugreek seeds, dry-toasted and crushed using a pestle and mortar
3 tablespoons rose harissa
3 kaffir lime leaves
2 teaspoons turmeric
4 large garlic cloves, crushed
finely grated zest of 1 unwaxed lime
juice of ½ lime
2 tablespoons ghee or vegetable oil
Maldon sea salt flakes and freshly ground black pepper

Line a large baking tray with baking paper.

Combine the marinade ingredients in a bowl, season generously with salt and pepper, then blend together to form a smooth paste.

Cut 3 slashes on the top of the lamb leg and a couple more on the underside of the joint. Place the meat on the prepared baking tray, then massage the paste into the meat, especially the slashes and bone areas. Leave the meat to marinate in the refrigerator overnight or, if you are pushed for time, for a minimum of 1 hour.

Preheat the oven to 220°C (200°C fan), Gas Mark 7. Put the lamb in the oven and immediately reduce the temperature to 190°C (170°C fan), Gas Mark 5. Roast for about 1 hour, or until the flesh takes on a nice pink colour. If you prefer your lamb slightly more cooked, increase the cooking time by 20 minutes. You can also slow-cook this joint at 180°C, 160°C (fan), Gas Mark 4, for 4 hours – check after 3 hours and if necessary cover the meat with kitchen foil to prevent burning, for a tender, fully cooked result.

Cover the leg of lamb loosely with kitchen foil and leave to rest for 10 minutes before serving.

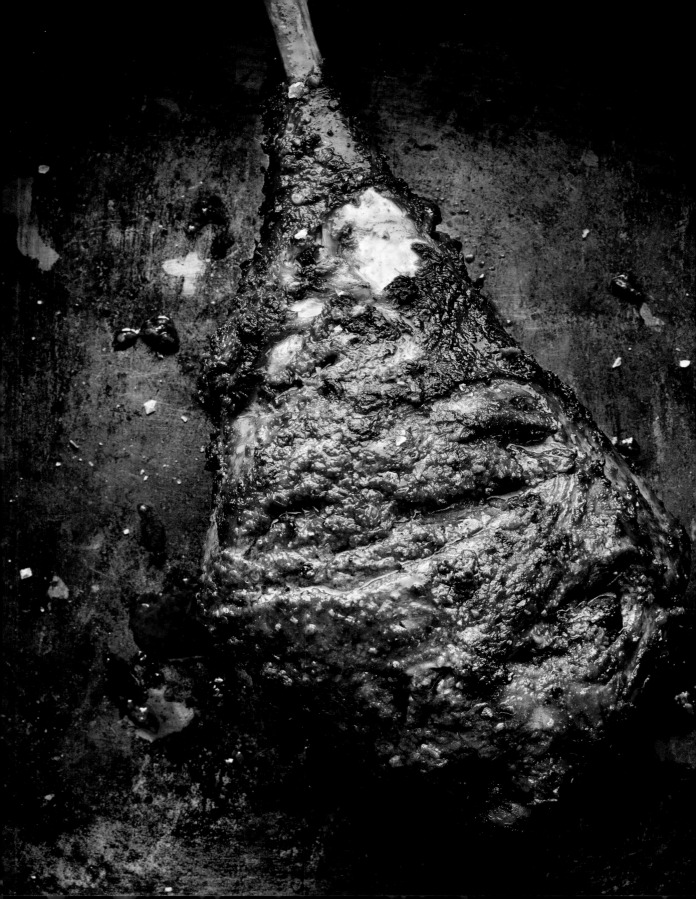

LAMB, PLUM & PRESERVED LEMON STEW

vegetable oil

2 large onions, roughly chopped

800g lamb neck, cut into chunks

2 handfuls of dried fenugreek leaves

100g fresh coriander, finely chopped

100g flat leaf parsley, finely chopped

6 plums, halved and pitted

8 preserved lemons, halved and deseeded

Maldon sea salt flakes and freshly ground black pepper

Set a large saucepan or casserole over medium heat and drizzle in a generous amount of oil. When the oil is hot, add the onion and fry for 6–8 minutes, or until translucent and the edges start to brown. Add the diced lamb and cook, stirring frequently, for a few minutes to seal it without browning, then season well with salt and pepper. Stir in the dried fenugreek leaves, ensuring the lamb is well coated in them (add more oil if you need it), then add the fresh herbs and stir-fry for 12–15 minutes, or until the herbs have completely wilted, reduced in volume and lost their bright green colour.

Pour in enough boiling water to just cover all the ingredients, then reduce the heat to low. Cook for 2 hours, stirring occasionally. Add the plum halves and cook for a further 45 minutes.

Stir in the preserved lemon halves and season to taste. Cook for a further 5 minutes to heat through. If not serving straight away, leave the stew to cool completely, then refrigerate (see tip). Gently reheat the stew and serve alongside plain basmati rice.

TIP

This stew is at its best and even more delicious when made the day before you serve it. You can also substitute pork neck for the lamb.

SPICY BEEF NOODLES

with green beans

SERVES 6-8

500g minced beef (15 per cent fat)

200g salted peanuts

400g flat rice noodles (about 1cm wide)

vegetable oil

1 large head of garlic, cloves bashed and thinly sliced

2 teaspoons ground cumin

1 teaspoon ground cinnamon

400g trimmed green beans, cut into 2.5cm pieces

4 tablespoons light tahini

2-3 tablespoons rose harissa

1 bunch of spring onions, thinly sliced from root to tip

1 small bunch (about 30g) of fresh coriander, finely chopped

Maldon sea salt flakes and freshly ground black pepper

Remove the mince from the refrigerator and leave to come up to room temperature.

Heat a large frying pan over a medium-high heat. When hot, add the peanuts and dry-toast for 5-6 minutes, or until they start to blacken in parts but not all over. Transfer to a bowl and set aside.

Rinse the noodles under cold running water – I find this prevents them from sticking together during cooking. Drain in a colander.

Put the noodles into a large saucepan set over a high heat and add enough boiling water to generously cover the noodles. Cook according to the packet instructions or to your preference. Reserve 2 large cupfuls of the cooking liquid for making the sauce, then rinse the noodles under cold running water. Drain, then return the noodles to the pan and set aside.

Meanwhile, pour just enough oil into the frying pan you used to toast the peanuts to coat the base of the pan. Heat the oil over a medium heat, then add the mince and break it down with a wooden spoon as quickly as possible to avoid clumping. Add the garlic, cumin and cinnamon and stir-fry until the beef turns brown and is starting to crisp on the edges. Stir in the green beans and fry for a further 5 minutes. Lastly, add the tahini and rose harissa, season with a generous amount of salt and pepper and stir in a little cold water to thin out and loosen the mixture, if needed, to prevent the tahini from thickening.

Tip the beef mixture into the pan containing the noodles. Add a cup of the reserved noodle-cooking liquid and mix well until incorporated. If, like me, you like a brothy dish you can add the second cup of cooking water. Check the seasoning. Mix in the spring onions and coriander and serve, garnished with the charred peanuts.

CARDAMOM &
COCONUT DHAL

with turmeric & nigella seeds

SERVES 6

2 teaspoons cumin seeds

2 teaspoons coriander seeds

2 black cardamom pods

seeds from 7 green cardamom pods

2 teaspoons fennel seeds

2 tablespoons ghee or vegetable oil, plus extra as needed

2 onions, finely chopped

5 fat garlic cloves, crushed

7.5–10cm fresh turmeric, finely grated or 1 heaped teaspoon ground turmeric powder

500g red lentils

50g desiccated coconut

400ml can coconut milk

50g salted butter

Maldon sea salt flakes and freshly ground black pepper

TO GARNISH

2 tomatoes, diced

1 red onion, finely chopped

½ small bunch (about 15g) of fresh coriander, chopped

2 teaspoons nigella seeds

Heat a large frying pan over a medium-high heat, add the cumin seeds, coriander seeds, black cardamom pods, green cardamom seeds and the fennel seeds and dry-toast for about 2 minutes, shaking the pan until they release their aroma and begin to brown a little, taking care not to let them burn. Set aside the black cardamom pods, then crush the remaining toasted spices using a pestle and mortar.

Return the crushed spices to the pan. Increase the heat to medium-high. Add the ghee or oil to the spices, then add the onions and fry for about 6 minutes, then add the garlic and fry for 1 minute, stirring to ensure it does not burn. Add the grated turmeric (or ground turmeric powder) and fry for 1–2 minutes, or until the onions are soft.

Add the lentils and desiccated coconut to the saucepan (and a little more ghee or oil, if the pan looks dry). Stir well, ensuring they are coated in the onion, spice and ghee mixture. Cook, stirring, for 1–2 minutes, then pour in the coconut milk and add the toasted black cardamom pods. Top up with enough water to completely cover the contents of the pan. Season well with salt and pepper.

Bring to the boil, then cover the pan with a lid, reduce the heat to low and simmer for about 45 minutes, stirring occasionally to prevent sticking. Check the liquid level from time to time – if the liquid is being absorbed too quickly, add a little more water. If the liquid level seems too high, increase the heat level and remove the pan lid to reduce liquid volumes in the pan.

Just before serving, discard the black cardamom pods, then stir in the butter. Serve garnished with the tomatoes, red onion, fresh coriander and a sprinkling of nigella seeds.

SPICED POTATOES

with garlic chips & turmeric yogurt

SERVES 4–8 AS A SIDE

700g waxy potatoes, such as Fingerling, Anya or Charlotte, halved lengthways

extra virgin olive oil

finely grated zest of 1 unwaxed lemon

2 teaspoons cumin seeds

1–1½ teaspoons chilli flakes

1 tablespoon coarse black pepper

ghee or vegetable oil

Maldon sea salt flakes and freshly ground black pepper

FOR THE TURMERIC YOGURT

200ml Greek yogurt

extra virgin olive oil

7.5cm piece of fresh turmeric, finely grated

1 small bunch (about 30g) mint, leaves stripped, rolled up tightly and thinly sliced into ribbons

6 fat garlic cloves, bashed, thinly sliced and fried into garlic crisps

Bring a large saucepan of water to the boil. Add the potatoes and parboil them for about 10 minutes, or until the potatoes are almost cooked but still firm in the centres (use a skewer or knife to check this). Drain and rinse the potatoes, then pat them dry, put them into a bowl and leave to dry. When dry, drizzle a little extra virgin olive oil into the bowl and add the lemon zest, cumin seeds, chilli flakes and pepper. Toss to coat the potato halves well with this mixture.

Pour enough ghee or vegetable oil into a large frying pan to generously coat the base and set it over a medium heat. When the oil is hot, add the potatoes with their cut sides facing downwards. Fry them slowly for 8–10 minutes on each side, or until the potatoes have a deep golden crust on them. (Alternatively, roast them at 220°C, 200°C (fan), Gas Mark 7, for 35–40 minutes if you prefer.) Transfer the potatoes to a platter and season well with salt.

Meanwhile, season the yogurt with salt and pepper and stir in a little olive oil. Mix the grated turmeric loosely into the yogurt, swirling it to give a marbled effect.

Scatter the mint and crispy garlic chips over the fried potatoes, and serve with the turmeric yogurt.

FREEKEH, TOMATO & CHICKPEA PILAF

2 tablespoons cumin seeds

olive oil

4 large onions, 1 diced and 3 halved and
  very thinly sliced into half-moons

2 tablespoons tomato purée

400g freekeh

50g unsalted butter

400g can chopped tomatoes

400g can chickpeas, drained

400ml chicken or vegetable stock

200ml water

vegetable oil

Maldon sea salt flakes and freshly ground
  black pepper

TO GARNISH

150ml Greek yogurt

handful of chopped coriander or parsley

Heat a large frying pan over a medium-high heat, add the cumin seeds and dry-toast for about 2 minutes, shaking the pan until they release their aroma and begin to brown a little, taking care not to let them burn.

Add a drizzle of olive oil to the pan, add the diced onion and fry for 6–8 minutes, or until softened. Add the tomato purée and dissolve it into the onion mixture, adding a little more oil if needed, then add the freekeh and butter and stir well until the freekeh is evenly coated in the onion mixture and the butter has melted. Stir-fry for 1 minute, then add the canned tomatoes and chickpeas and mix well.

Pour in the stock and the water and season with a generous amount of salt and pepper. Cover the saucepan with a lid, reduce the heat to low and cook for 20–25 minutes without disturbing the pan. Remove the pan from the heat and set aside, leaving the lid on.

Meanwhile, prepare the fried onions for a garnish. Line a plate with a double layer of kitchen paper. Pour enough vegetable oil into a saucepan to fill it to a depth of 1cm and heat over a high heat. Add the sliced onion and fry for 8–10 minutes, or until golden brown and crispy – avoid stirring or they will start to caramelize. Remove the fried onions with a metal slotted spoon and transfer to the paper-lined plate to drain.

Add half the fried onions to the freekeh and, using a fork, gently comb through the freekeh to stir in the onions and fluff up the grains and chickpeas. Arrange the freekeh mixture on a wide, flat platter. Dot with the yogurt and scatter the remaining fried onions and coriander or parsley on top. This is also good drizzled with your favourite chilli sauce.

TIP

To make this a vegan recipe, omit the butter, and substitute coconut or soya yogurt for the Greek yogurt.

WHITE CHOCOLATE, CARDAMOM & MACADAMIA SQUARES

MAKES 9

2 large eggs

150g unsalted butter, melted (or 150ml oil, if you prefer), plus extra for greasing

50g light muscovado sugar

150g golden caster sugar

seeds from 6 cardamom pods, finely ground using a pestle and mortar

2 teaspoons ground ginger

finely grated zest of 1 unwaxed orange

225g plain flour

200g white chocolate, melted

75g macadamia nuts, halved

pouring cream, to serve

Preheat the oven to 200°C (180°C fan), Gas Mark 6. Grease a 21cm square brownie or cake tin and line with baking paper.

Beat the eggs, melted butter or oil and sugars together in a large mixing bowl until the mixture is smooth. Add the ground cardamom seeds, ground ginger and orange zest and mix well. Blend in the flour until the mixture is smooth. Mix in the white chocolate and blend again until smooth, then finally fold in the macadamia nuts.

Pour the mixture into the prepared tin. Bake for 25–30 minutes, or until set on top – they should still be a bit gooey inside. During the last few minutes of the cooking time, prepare a shallow sink with iced or cold water to extend halfway up the sides of your cake tin. When the cake is baked, plunge the tin into the water, making sure no water enters the tin – this will stop the cooking process and will leave you with a nice fudgy centre. Leave the tin to sit in the cold water until the cake is completely cool. Cut into 9 squares and serve with pouring cream.

TIP

If making this treat the night before serving, keep refrigerated until ready to serve.

DOUGHNUT FRITTERS

with cinnamon-orange sugar

MAKES 20-24

FOR THE DOUGHNUT FRITTERS
250g plain flour
1 teaspoon baking powder
pinch of Maldon sea salt flakes
350ml boiling water
50g unsalted butter, melted
vegetable oil

FOR THE SPICED SUGAR
200g caster sugar
finely grated zest of 2 unwaxed oranges
2 teaspoons ground cinnamon

First, prepare the spiced sugar. Mix the sugar, orange zest and cinnamon in a shallow bowl. Cover with clingfilm and set aside.

To make the fritters, sift the flour, baking powder and a good pinch of salt into a mixing bowl and make a well in the centre. Pour the boiling water into a measuring jug and stir in the melted butter. Pour the mixture into the flour and combine quickly to make a sticky dough. Leave to rest for 10 minutes.

Pour enough oil into a large, deep saucepan to fill to a depth of about 5cm. Bring the oil to a frying temperature (add a pinch of dough: if it immediately bubbles gently, then the oil is at the right temperature). Meanwhile, line a tray with kitchen paper.

Using a metal teaspoon, scoop up a spoonful of dough. Push it off the spoon and carefully into the hot oil. Repeat until the pan is almost full, ensuring there are not too many in the pan to avoid them sticking together. Fry for 3–4 minutes on each side, or until deep golden brown. (If the fritters brown too quickly, the oil may be too hot – reduce the heat slightly if this happens.) When cooked, transfer the fritters to the paper-lined tray to drain any excess oil, then roll each fritter in the spiced sugar to coat. Repeat with the remaining sough, then serve immediately.

TIP

To make this a vegan recipe, substitute light olive oil for the butter.

ADDITIONAL MENU IDEAS

VEGAN FEAST

Pomegranate & aubergine salad
(see page 52)

Charred cauliflower
(see page 193)

Cardamom & coconut dhal
with turmeric & nigella seeds
(see page 223)

Freekeh, tomato & chickpea pilaf
(see page 227)

Doughnut fritters with
cinnamon-orange sugar
(see page 230)

PERFECT PICNICS

Pea pastizzi (see page 26)

Tomato & olive salad with
za'atar & buttermilk dressing
(see page 57)

Orzo & tomato salad
(see page 142)

Aubergine rolls with goats' cheese,
herbs & walnuts (see page 162)

Cauliflower, anari, black pepper
& thyme quiches (see page 210)

Blackberry & apple sandwiches
(see page 198)

CASUAL FOOD WITH FRIENDS

Goats' cheese & filo pies with orange, pistachio & oregano (see page 17)

Ultimate chicken shawarmas (see page 73)

Harissa skirt steak sandwiches (see page 75)

Grilled corn in harissa mayo with feta, mint, coriander & chilli (see page 132)

Lamb kofta roll (see page 215)

Blueberry, lime & ginger cheesecakes (see page 145)

HEARTY FAMILY FOOD

Chicken, pistachio & black pepper curry (see page 42)

Green bean & tomato stew (see page 113)

Garlic, fenugreek & cumin flatbreads (see page 115)

Spiced lamb hotpot (see page 180)

Banana, coffee & chocolate chunk cake with salted caramel & peanut butter sundae top (see page 119)

INDEX

ACKNOWLEDGEMENTS

To my agent and friend, Martine Carter at Sauce Management, who has the patience of a saint and who I can always rely on for the truth, thank you for helping my career to blossom. To my brilliant publisher Stephanie Jackson at Octopus, who I call a friend. To the legend who is Caroline Brown, Publicity Director at Octopus, and her entire team, specifically Ellen, Matt and Siobhan who do so much to provide essential support to every book I write and guide me through the process so fluidly.

A special thanks to the wonderful creative team behind the book: the brilliant and lovely Kris Kirkham, who just 'gets' the mad inner-workings of my brain and loves food as much as I do, his assistant Hannah Hughes, and my good friends, the lovely Food Stylist Laura Field and Home Economist Kim Somauroo for taking on my food and making it all look beautiful and taste delicious for the shoot – it was a pleasure to bake 'cake of the day'!

To Sybella Stephens, Jazzy Fizzle, Jonathan Christie, Peter Hunt and Fran Johnson for all your magic taking my words and visions and turning them into spectacular creations every time. A big thank you to Tim Hely Hutchinson, Alison Goff and Denise Bates for always supporting me and making me feel like a valued part of the Octopus family, and a big huge thank you to Kevin Hawkins and everyone at Octopus who work so tirelessly to promote, distribute and support each book I write.

A huge thank you to Belazu – kind, hard-working and razor-sharp as well as the most wonderful (and ridiculously fun) bunch of people you could ever hope to meet. Thank you for the excellent ingredients that led to me creating so many wonderful meals and now three lovely books.

A heartfelt thank you to all the friends and loved ones who have cared for me, laughed and cried with me, been patient with me and supported, comforted and educated me at one time or another in my life… to think that any of my achievements were possible without your contributions to my life would, quite frankly, be utterly preposterous.

And again, last, but by no means least, my lovely Mum, who supports, loves, encourages, comforts and pretty much does everything – except cook for me – thank you, more than ever, I realize how lucky I am to call you my Mother and even more a friend.